THE CHILD'S
STORY BIBLE:
OLD TESTAMENT

Volume 2—1 Samuel to Malachi

The Philistines could not fight in such a storm. 1 Samuel 7

The Child's Story Bible:
Old Testament

Volume 2—1 Samuel to Malachi

Catherine F. Vos

*New edition
illustrated in full colour
by Betty Beeby*

THE BANNER OF TRUTH TRUST

THE BANNER OF TRUTH TRUST
3 Murrayfield Road, Edinburgh EH12 6EL
PO Box 621, Carlisle, Pennsylvania 17013, USA

*

THE CHILD'S STORY BIBLE
by CATHERINE F. VOS

*Vol. 1, November, 1934
Vol. 2, October, 1935
Vol. 3, October, 1936
One-volume edition, April, 1940
Second edition, August, 1949
Third edition, May, 1958
Fourth edition, October, 1969*

*This English edition is published by special arrangement with
Wm. B. Eerdmans Publishing Company
Grand Rapids, Michigan, U.S.A.*
1969

*New Testament only
Reprinted 1976*

*Old Testament Vol 1 : Genesis to Ruth 1977
Old Testament Vol 2: 1 Samuel to Malachi 1977*

ISBN 0 85151 251 8

Printed in Great Britain
Photo-litho reprint by W & J Mackay Limited, Chatham
from earlier impression

Dedication

To My Dear Mother in Heaven,
Who Told Me These Stories
When I Was a Little Child,
In Much the Same Way
In Which I Have Written Them
In This Book.

Foreword

Retelling Bible stories is both a painstaking and a rewarding task. By the use of simple and dignified language the author, Mrs. Catherine F. Vos, has in her book preserved the beauty of the biblical narratives and at the same time skilfully brought out the meaning of the scriptural account. Her picturesque, imaginative, and poetic style is in harmony with the dignity of the message.

For such reasons the *Child's Story Bible* is one of the most widely known and used Bible story books. The National Union of Christian Schools is happy to have had a hand in the preparation of this book, which was originally intended for use in the Christian schools. Teachers use it for Bible instruction in primary and intermediate grades.

Parents find that the material is adapted also for home use: for reading to the children and also for placing in their hands for personal reading. Although it is intended primarily for children from seven to twelve years of age, it is eminently suitable for reading to those of a much younger age and it is valued by adults as a Bible history.

The publishers spared no expense to make this volume beautiful and to make it appealing to the child. Large, readable type and full-colour art work, help to make it an attractive book. A new element in this edition is the reproduction of several oil paintings of principal Bible characters.

Telling the story of salvation to those who come after us is a glorious task. Christian faith has its roots in historical events. We trust that the *Child's Story Bible* may be a guide to the authoritative narration of these events, the Book of books, and to Him who said, "I am the way, the truth, and the life."

JOHN A. VANDER ARK, *Director*
National Union of Christian Schools

TABLE OF CONTENTS

Old Testament: 1 Samuel to Malachi

CHAPTER 65

Samuel Is Promised to God

I Samuel 1, 2, 3

Part 1 — Hannah's Prayer

There was living in Israel a man named Elkanah. He had two wives, as a great many people in those days had. As often happened, Elkanah's having two wives caused trouble in the family. One wife, Peninnah, received a number of children; but Hannah, whom Elkanah loved more, had none.

In those days, every wife wanted very much to have many children. It was a great disgrace for her not to have any. Hannah's disappointment was the worse because Peninnah was very proud of her fine family. She was always boasting about her children, while poor Hannah had none.

Hannah became very unhappy. Many a day she went off all by herself and cried bitterly because God had not given her any children.

Elkanah was a good man, who brought up his family in the fear of God. Every year he took his wives and children to Shiloh to worship the Lord in the Tabernacle.

Even there Peninnah jeered at Hannah, for she was jealous that her husband loved Hannah more. Poor Hannah could not keep her tears from falling when she heard Peninnah's taunts.

Her husband tried to comfort her, for he could not bear to see her unhappy. "Never mind, Hannah," he said. "Don't cry any more. Don't you know that I love you more than ten sons could? Dry your eyes, my dear, and don't grieve. Come and eat your dinner."

Hannah had made up her mind what to do. After dinner was over, she left the others and went to the temple of the Lord.

There she saw the priest of the temple, Eli, sitting on a seat by the door of the temple.

Hannah began to pray to the Lord, asking Him to give her a son. She promised that she would give him back to the Lord to serve Him all the days of his life, and that as a sign of this promise his hair would never be cut.

Hannah prayed earnestly to God from her heart. Only her lips moved. When the old priest Eli saw her lips moving without a sound, he thought she was drunk. He called out to her, "How long are you going to be drunk? Put away your wine."

Hannah was very much surprised to have Eli speak to her so. "Oh, no, my lord, I am not drunk," she replied. "I am a sorrowful woman and I have been praying to the Lord to help me. Please do not think that I am a bad woman. I have been telling the Lord my trouble, and asking Him to help me."

"Go in peace," said Eli, "and the God of Israel give you what you have asked."

After this, Hannah felt certain that God would give her the son that she had prayed for. She went back to her husband comforted, and her face was happy and peaceful.

The next morning, Elkanah brought his whole family to the temple to worship the Lord. Then they went back to Ramah, where they lived. Before long the Lord sent Hannah the son she had prayed for. She named him Samuel, which means *Asked of God*.

The next year, when Elkanah took his family to Shiloh to worship the Lord, Hannah did not go, for the baby was too young. She said to her husband, "I shall not go to Shiloh with you, till the baby is older. Then I will bring him to the Lord so that he may live there forever."

When little Samuel was four or five years old, Hannah went with the rest of them to worship the Lord at Shiloh. She and her husband took the little boy to Eli, the old priest. Hannah said to him, "O my lord, truly I am the woman who was praying here in the temple. It was for this child I prayed, and God has given me what I asked for. Now I have given him to the Lord. As long as he lives, he shall be lent to the Lord."

Hannah left her little boy with Eli to be brought up in the temple. He helped the old priest.

Every year, when Elkanah brought his family to Shiloh to worship the Lord, Hannah came to see her little boy. Each year she brought him a little coat which she had made. Oh, how eagerly Hannah looked forward to the days when she could see her precious son again! How proud she was of him, when she saw how tall he had grown! She was still prouder when she saw how nicely he was learning to wait upon Eli, whose eyes were dim with age.

Eli blessed Elkanah and his wife, saying, "May the Lord give you more children to reward you for lending this child to Him." God did reward Hannah by giving her three more little boys and two little girls.

PART 2 — THE VOICE OF GOD

Eli was a very old man. He had two sons named Hophni and Phineas, grown-up men. I am sorry to say that though the old priest, Eli, was a good man, his two sons were just the opposite. They behaved in such a shameful way that all the people of Israel were shocked at their wickedness. The priest Eli could not live much longer, and the people dreaded what would happen when his wicked sons should become priests in his place.

As little boys, they had been very naughty. Their father had been much too gentle with them, and had not made them behave well, as he should have. Since they were not punished when they were children, they grew up to be very bad men. Their father talked to them about this, but they would not listen to him.

God sent a prophet to Eli with bad news. God had said that the descendants of Aaron should be His priests forever. But now, since Eli had permitted his sons to become so wicked, God would not let his family be priests. Both his sons would die on the same day. From that time on, there would never be an old man in Eli's family. All his descendants would die young. God would appoint another priest, who would be a good man.

Too late, Eli learned that God always holds parents responsible for the way in which they bring up their children. When your father and mother correct you for some fault, remember that they are only doing their duty.

One evening little Samuel went to bed as usual. He awoke from his sleep, thinking he heard Eli calling him. He ran to the old priest and said, "Here I am, for you called me."

But Eli thought Samuel had been dreaming. He said, "I did not call you. Lie down again, and go back to sleep."

Samuel went back to bed. Soon he heard his name called again. "Samuel! Samuel!" He jumped up again, and ran to Eli, saying, "Here I am, for you called me."

Again Eli said, "No, my boy, I did not call you. Lie down again, and go to sleep."

Samuel went back to bed once more. Before long he heard the same voice calling "Samuel!"

Eli finally saw that it must be the Lord who had called Samuel, and he said, "Go and lie down, and if the Lord calls you again, say 'Speak, Lord, for your servant hears.'"

When Samuel heard the voice of the Lord calling again, "Samuel, Samuel!" he said "Speak, Lord, for your servant hears."

Then God told Samuel that He was going to send a terrible punishment on Eli, because Eli had not punished his sons to turn them away from their wickedness.

Samuel lay still until the morning. He got up and opened the doors of the temple as usual. He did not dare to tell Eli what God had said to him.

But Eli called him. "What did the Lord say to you? Tell me the whole truth. Do not hide anything that the Lord said to you."

Then Samuel told him everything that God had said. Eli himself was a very good man. His only fault was that he had not controlled his wicked sons. He said, "It is the Lord. Let Him do what seems good to Him."

Samuel stayed with Eli. As he grew older, it became plainer and plainer that God was with him. God often spoke to Samuel. All Israel, from the far north to the south, knew that God was making Samuel His prophet.

CHAPTER 66

War With the Philistines

I SAMUEL 4-8

PART 1 — BAD NEWS

As you remember, Samson killed many of the Philistines in his life-time, and conquered them to such an extent that they did not again trouble the Israelites for a long time. But Samson had been dead now for many a year, and the Philistines had increased and become strong.

The Israelites fought against them and were badly beaten. About four thousand of the Israelite soldiers were killed.

The elders said to each other, "Why has God let us be defeated today by the Philistines? Next time, let us take the Ark of the Covenant out of the Tabernacle into the battlefield with us. Then God will give us the victory."

What was wrong with this plan? Do you not remember that the golden Ark was very sacred? It was kept in the Holy of Holies, where no one was allowed to enter, except the high priest when he made atonement for the sins of the people once a year. Even when the Israelites journeyed, the Ark was covered, so that no one was able to see it.

And now the people were taking the sacred Ark out of the Tabernacle and carrying it to the battlefield! Besides, those who carried the Ark to battle were Eli's wicked sons!

When the Ark was brought into the camp, the people set up such a great shout that the earth echoed with the sound. The Philistines heard the noise and asked, "Why are the Israelites shouting so loudly?"

Someone told them that the Ark of God had been brought into the camp. The Philistines were filled with terror. Such a thing had never happened before! Who should deliver them out of the hand of the Israelites? "These," they said, "are the gods that smote the Egyptians with those terrible plagues."

You see, they did not even know that the Israelites had only one God. They thought they had many gods, like themselves. They expected to lose the battle, but they were too brave to run away.

The Philistines fought courageously. And they defeated the Israelites. Eli's two sons, Hophni and Phineas, were killed. And the Philistines took the Ark.

A man of Israel ran out of the army to Shiloh, to tell the people what had happened. To show his grief for the great defeat, he tore his clothes and put earth upon his head.

When this newsbearer told the people of Shiloh the sad story, the whole city raised a bitter cry.

Blind old Eli was sitting on a seat by the side of the road, waiting for news of the battle. He was so anxious that he trembled all over. Had some harm come to God's holy Ark? He heard the people crying, and asked, "What does all this noise mean?"

The man came to him and said, "I have run out of the army. There has been a hard battle. The Israelites have been beaten. Many of them have been killed. Your sons Hophni and Phineas are dead. The Ark of God has been captured."

Poor old Eli listened with fear to the sad news. God had punished his sons for their wickedness. But when the messenger said that the Ark of God was captured, that was too much for Eli. He fell over backward, his neck was broken, and he died.

PART 2 — THE STORY OF THE ARK

The Philistines took the Ark to one of their cities, called Ashdod. In Ashdod was a temple of the fish-god Dagon. The Philistines brought the Ark into the temple and set it beside the idol.

In the morning, when they went into the temple, they found that Dagon had fallen down upon his face in front of the Ark of God.

They took up the image and set it in its place. But the next morning they found that Dagon had fallen down again. This time his hands and his head were broken off. There was nothing left but a stump, for the lower part of Dagon was merely a fish's tail.

The people of the city became ill, and many of them died. They said, "We won't have the Ark of the God of Israel stay with us any more, for He is hurting us and our god Dagon."

The men of Ashdod called a meeting of all the lords of the Philistines to decide what they should do with the Ark. They sent it to Gath, which was another city of the Philistines. But God sent a sickness like boils to the people of Gath. Many of them died, too.

The Ark stayed seven months in the country of the Philistines. The Lord visited the people with sickness and plagues, so that many of them died wherever the Ark was.

They were afraid to have the Ark of God with them any longer, but they did not know what to do with it. They called some of their heathen priests and magicians to settle the problem.

These men said that if the Ark were sent back to the Israelites, some presents should be sent with it to give glory to the God of Israel. Did they not remember how the Egyptians had suffered when they hardened their hearts?

The magicians advised the people to make a new cart, and hitch to it two cows whose young calves had been taken away from them. The presents and the Ark should be placed on the cart. Then the cart should be set on the road to Beth-shemesh, which is in the country of the Israelites. If the cows should go right along to Beth-shemesh, then the Philistines might know that it was the Lord who sent this sickness. If the cows should turn back to their calves, then the Philistines might know that it was not the Lord, but that the sickness just happened to come.

The Philistines followed this plan. And when the cart was set on the road to Beth-shemesh, the cows never once looked behind. They went straight along the road, lowing as they went. The lords of the Philistines followed them till they came to Beth-shemesh.

It was just the time of the wheat harvest. All the people of the town were in the wheat fields, reaping the harvest. They saw the Ark of the Covenant of their God coming down the road, and all the lords of the Philistines following. How glad they were to see it!

Some Levites, the only ones who had any right to touch the Ark of the Covenant, took the Ark from the cart. They put it, with the box of presents, upon a great stone that was standing there. Then they offered burnt offerings and sacrifices to the Lord.

But the Israelites of Beth-shemesh did a very wrong thing. Many of them came to the stone where the Ark was resting. They opened the lid with the two golden cherubim carved on it, and looked inside the Ark. That was wrong, for no one was allowed to touch the Ark except the Levites. God punished them immediately, sending death to many of them.

Then the people were afraid to keep the Ark in Beth-shemesh. They sent word to the people of another town, Kirjath-jearim, asking them to take the Ark to their city.

The men of Kirjath-jearim carried the Ark to their city. It remained there for twenty years.

PART 3 — SAMUEL AS JUDGE

Samuel was now a man. He had been a good boy, and he became a good man. Everybody respected and loved him; and God loved him, too.

Eli had judged Israel for forty years. After his death Samuel became the judge. God spoke to Samuel as He had spoken to Moses and Aaron.

It was a great comfort to Israel to know that God was again speaking to His people through a prophet. Many of the Israelites had turned to idolatry, but now they remembered that they were God's people, and they longed to come back to the Lord and worship Him only.

Samuel promised that if they would put away their heathen idols and worship Jehovah, He would take them back again and deliver them from the Philistines. The Israelites were glad to leave their idols.

Samuel called a gathering of all the people at Mizpeh. They must confess their sins to God and ask Him to forgive them. For a whole day they fasted, confessing their sin. All day long, Samuel prayed for them.

When the Philistines heard of this great meeting, they thought it would be a good chance to make war. Collecting their soldiers, they went toward Mizpeh.

The children of Israel were very much frightened. They asked Samuel not to stop praying for them. Samuel prayed, offering up a lamb for a burnt offering As he was offering the lamb, the Lord began to help the Israelites.

The heavens grew black, the winds blew, the rain came pouring down. Peal after peal of the most awe-inspiring thunder rent the sky. Great streaks of vivid lightning flashed across the heavens. The Philistines could not fight in such a storm. They became so confused that they broke their ranks and fled in terror.   The Israelites pursued them and won a victory.

Samuel took a great stone and set it up where the battle had been. He named the stone "Ebenezer," which means *Hitherto hath Jehovah helped us.*

The Philistines were so badly beaten that as long as Samuel lived they never again troubled the Israelites.   They even gave up the cities that they had taken away from the Israelites. Ekron and Gath and the other cities of the sea-coast belonged to Israel again.

Every year Samuel journeyed to Bethel, to Gilgal, and to Mizpeh, returning again to his own city of Ramah. He judged the people of Israel in all these places.

The people no longer worshipped idols. They served the Lord and were very peaceful and happy while Samuel was their judge.

After many years, Samuel became an old man. He made his two sons judges over Israel.   Because these sons were not as good as Samuel, they did not judge the people justly.

The elders of the people came to Samuel and asked him to give them a king to rule over them, like the other nations. Samuel was not pleased, but he did not know what to answer. He did what all good men ought to do when they are in trouble—he prayed to the Lord.

God told him to listen to the people. They should not have asked for a king, for Jehovah was their ruler.   They would be sorry that they had ever asked to be like the other nations. But God would give them a king.

Samuel told the people that their king would take their sons and daughters to serve him. He would take away their fields to give to his favorites. They would have to pay heavy taxes.

But even when Samuel warned them that they would soon be sorry, the people wanted their own way, to have a king like the other nations.

CHAPTER 67

Saul, the First King

I SAMUEL 9-15

PART 1 — CHOSEN BY GOD

In the tribe of Benjamin there was a rich man named Kish who had a son named Saul. In the whole land of Israel, there was not a finer, more handsome young man than Saul. He was a whole head taller than any other young man in the entire kingdom.

Saul's father had a great many asses. One day some asses, which had been turned loose in a field to graze, wandered away and were lost. Saul's father said to his son, "Take one of the servants with you, and go out to look for the asses."

Saul and the servant started out. They hunted all through Mount Ephraim, but they did not find the asses. They went all through the land of Benjamin without finding a trace of the missing animals.

At last Saul said to the servant, "We had better go back, or my father will stop worrying about the asses and will begin worrying about us."

This was easier to say than to do. Saul and his servant had come so far from home that they could not find their way back. All at once the servant remembered that the prophet Samuel lived near the place where they now were. He would surely be able to tell them the way home.

As the two men set out to search for the house of the prophet, they met some young girls going to draw water. Saul asked, "Does the prophet live near here?"

"Yes," the young girls answered. "If you hurry you can find him easily, for there is a sacrifice today in the city. The people are waiting for him to come and bless the sacrifice before they sit down to eat."

Saul and his servant hurried on into the city. Soon they met Samuel himself, going up to the sacrifice.

Now, the very day before, God had spoken to Samuel and had said to him, "Tomorrow, about this time of day, I will send you a man out of the land of Benjamin. You are to anoint him to be king over My people Israel. He shall save them from the Philistines."

As Saul and his servant walked through the city in search of the prophet, God spoke again to Samuel and said, "This is the man that I told you of yesterday. He is the one who is to be king over My people."

At the same moment Saul came near to Samuel and said politely: "Tell me, I pray you, where the prophet lives."

Samuel answered, "I am the prophet." Then he invited Saul to spend the day with him. He added, "Tomorrow I will let you go home, and will tell you all that you want to know."

Although Saul had not yet mentioned the asses, Samuel said, "Do not be worried about the asses, for they are found." Then he said something which surprised Saul still more. "Are you not the man for whom all Israel is looking?" he asked.

Saul did not understand what Samuel meant. He said, "Why do you speak in this way? I am no one of importance."

Samuel did not yet tell Saul that God had chosen him to be king. He took him to the feast and made him sit in the highest seat of honor, and gave him the best of the food. Saul was very glad to get that fine dinner, for he and the servant had been wandering for three days in the hills, and all the food they had brought with them had been eaten.

Saul stayed with Samuel that day. The next morning Saul and his servant started to go home. Samuel went with them as far as the outskirts of the city. There he said to Saul, "Tell your servant to go ahead. You yourself must stay here a little while, till I can show you what God has said."

When the servant had gone on, Samuel took a bottle of anointing oil and emptied it over Saul's head. He kissed the young man, saying, "I have anointed you to be king over Israel, because God has chosen you to be captain over His people."

The prophet told Saul three things that would happen on the way home. First, two men would tell Saul that his father was worrying about him. Next, he would meet three men who would give him some bread. Finally, he would join a company of prophets.

All these signs came true, just as the prophet Samuel had said. Then Saul knew that he had been chosen by God, and he loved the Lord because God had given him a new heart.

A week later, Samuel sent word to all the tribes of Israel to come together. He wanted to announce the new king publicly. For many years the people had wanted to be ruled by a king, as other nations were ruled. They had not listened to Samuel's warning that in wanting a king they were rejecting God. At last God was giving them what they asked for.

When the people were come together, Samuel chose the tribe out of which the king must come. All the families of that tribe went near to Samuel, and the prophet chose one family. The men of that family approached Samuel, and the name of Saul, son of Kish, was called out. But Saul could not be found!

Saul knew, of course, that he would be chosen king, because Samuel had anointed him. He was so shy and modest, that he dared not face the people. He had hidden himself.

The people asked God what they should do. The answer came, "He has hidden himself among the baggage."

There the people found Saul. In triumph they brought him to Samuel. The prophet said to them, "See the man whom the Lord has chosen to be your king! There is no one like him among all the people."

Saul stood there, his head and shoulders above the crowd. When the Israelites saw the splendid, handsome young man who was to be their king, they went wild with joy. "Long live the king! Long live the king!" they shouted.

Part 2 — Saul Saves the Eyes of His People

As you remember, there were three tribes of Israelites who stayed on the eastern side of the Jordan River. These were the tribes of Gad, Reuben, and half of Manasseh.

The Ammonites had lived near this country, when the children of Israel first came into the land, after their forty years of wandering in the desert. God had commanded the Israelites not to fight with the Ammonites and not to take their land, because these people were the descendants of Lot, the nephew of Abraham.

The Ammonites still lived in that country. Their king Nahash was a very cruel and wicked man. He gathered an army and came against the peaceful town of Jabesh-gilead, one of the cities of Israel on the eastern side of the Jordan.

The people of Jabesh-gilead were frightened to see an army approaching. They tried to make peace with King Nahash, promising that if he would not kill them, they would willingly be his servants. But even this did not satisfy the heathen king. "I will promise not to fight you, if you will let me put out all your right eyes," he said.

The men of Jabesh-gilead heard these words with terror. They said to King Nahash, "Give us seven days to see if we can get some of of our nation to help us. If after seven days none of our friends will come, then we will let you put out our right eyes."

Messengers hurried to the city near which Saul was living, to ask for help. But the people of this city did not dare to fight against a powerful king, for they had no leader. They began to mourn and weep. What a dreadful thing was going to happen to the people of Jabesh-gilead!

Just then Saul came into town from his father's farm. He asked, "What is the matter? Why are all the people crying so loudly?" When he heard what was wrong, he became very angry. "Those wicked Ammonites!" he said. "I will show them they cannot put out the eyes of God's people!"

The spirit of God came upon Saul and made him brave. He took a yoke of oxen and cut them in pieces. Then he sent the pieces over all the land of Israel with this message: "Let all the people come out to help Saul and Samuel to fight against the Ammonites. If there is any man who will not come, his oxen shall be cut in pieces, as these have been."

All the men of Israel came quickly to Saul. Now that they had a leader, they were eager to help the people of Jabesh-gilead. Saul had an army of three hundred thirty thousand men.

Back to their homes went the men of Jabesh-gilead with the comforting message, "Tomorrow you shall have help." How glad the people of the little town were, when they heard the joyful news!

The next day, after dividing his soldiers into three companies, Saul hurried his army across the Jordan River to the city of Jabesh-gilead. The Israelites met the host of the Ammonites early in the morning. The army of Nahash was so badly beaten that there were not two men left together.

This great victory made Saul the hero of the people. They were ready to do anything for this handsome soldier who had led them so well.

Before the victory, all the people had not welcomed Saul. Some men had said openly that they did not want him to be king. When all the rest of the people had shouted "Long live the king!" these men had been silent. When all the rest of the people had brought gifts to their new leader, these men had said, "Saul will not be a good king."

Now, after Saul's splendid victory over the Ammonites, the rejoicing people said, "Where are those bad men who did not want Saul to be king? Bring them here, and let us kill them."

Saul said, "No, nobody shall be killed today, for today God has given us a great victory."

The people felt they must do something to show how delighted they were in their king. They went to Gilgal, where they sacrificed to God, who had given them the battle. Then they publicly made Saul king.

PART 3 — SAUL LOSES THE KINGDOM

You probably remember that when Moses led the host of the Israelites out of the land of Egypt through the desert, the cruel Amalekites followed after them and shot at the people who were too weak and old to keep up with the others.

Moses had sent Joshua out to fight with the Amalekites, while he himself went to the top of a hill and prayed. As long as Moses held up his hands, Israel won; but when his hands became so tired that he could hold them up no longer, then Amalek won. Aaron and Hur had held up Moses' hands, and Israel had won the battle. But the Lord was so angry with Amalek that He had promised to have war with them forever.

After Saul had reigned for a number of years over Israel, Samuel came to him with a message from God.

"The Lord once sent me to anoint you king over His people," the prophet said. "Now God wants you to go to war with the Amalekites and to destroy all that they have. Do not save anything."

Saul collected his soldiers and numbered them. There were two hundred ten thousand soldiers ready for war. With this army, Saul went south into the desert where the Amalekites lived.

There was a great battle which the Israelites won. Saul captured Agag, the king of the Amalekites, and killed all the people, as God had commanded. He and his soldiers did not obey God's commandment to kill all the animals, however. They kept all the good animals, destroying only what was not worth saving.

That night God spoke to Samuel in these words: "I am sorry that I ever made Saul king, for he has not obeyed Me."

This grieved Samuel. He cried to the Lord all night. The next morning he went to meet Saul, while it was still very early. The king met him with the words, "Blessed are you of the Lord! I have done all that God commanded me."

The king expected that Samuel would praise him. But the prophet asked, "Then why do I hear all these sheep bleating, and all these oxen lowing?"

"The people brought these from the Amalekites," Saul answered. "They saved the best of the sheep and the oxen to sacrifice to the Lord your God. We have utterly destroyed the rest, as the Lord said."

Then the old prophet said, "I shall tell you what the Lord said to me last night."

"I am listening," Saul replied.

Samuel went on. "You were not a great man, as you yourself know; yet did not God make you king over Israel? Why have you not obeyed Him? He told you to destroy utterly those sinners, the Amalekites. You have not done as the Lord told you to do."

Saul defended himself. "I have obeyed God. I have brought Agag, the king, here; but I have utterly destroyed all the people of the nation. It is true that my soldiers saved the best of the sheep and the oxen, although the Lord said they should be destroyed. But they brought them here for sacrifices to the Lord in Gilgal."

Samuel shook his head. "Do you think that the Lord is as well pleased with sacrifices as with obedience? To obey is better than sacrifice. Because you have disobeyed God, He will not let you and your your family be the kings of Israel."

Even now, Saul did not realize what he had done. "I have done wrong," he said, "but now go with me to worship the Lord."

He seemed to think that God would overlook his disobedience, and would forget to punish him. But Samuel said, "No, I will not go to worship the Lord with you, for you have disobeyed God. He will not let you be king."

As the prophet turned to go, Saul took hold of his robe, tearing the cloth. "In the same way as you tear this cloth, the Lord has torn the kingdom away from you and has given it to a neighbor of yours who is better than you are," predicted Samuel. Then he ordered, "Bring Agag to me."

The Amalekite king came with a light step, for he said to himself, "Since they have saved my life so long, they will surely not kill me now."

But Samuel said, "As your sword has made women childless, so shall your mother be made childless." With these words the prophet killed Agag.

Samuel went home to his house at Ramah. He never again came to see Saul, as long as he lived. He mourned because Saul had proved himself to be so bad a leader for God's people.

CHAPTER 68

David, the Shepherd Boy

I SAMUEL 16, 17

PART 1 — A SHEPHERD BECOMES KING

For a while we shall leave Saul and his wars. Let us take a walk over the hills of Judah. Let us start at the little town of Bethlehem, where Ruth lived with her husband many years ago.

Do you see that fine house upon the hill? That is the house of Ruth and Boaz, which they built nearly a hundred years ago. They are dead now. Their son Obed is dead, too. Obed's son Jesse is living there with his family of eight sons, in the place where his grandfather Boaz and his grandmother Ruth once lived.

It is springtime. There are flowers on every side. The brook which flows through the meadows murmurs softly over the stones.

Oh, see those little snow-white lambs! How many there are! The sheep are nibbling the soft grass. Let us sit a while on this green hillside and watch them.

Listen! Did you hear that sweet sound? There it comes again. What is it? It must be a shepherd boy singing.

There he is, sitting down under that oak tree. He cannot see us, because we are behind some bushes. Listen!

> "Jehovah is my Shepherd;
> I shall not want.
> He maketh me to lie down in green pastures.
> He leadeth me beside still waters."

The stone sank down deep into Goliath's forehead. 1 Samuel 17

David walked quietly to the place where Saul lay. 1 Samuel 23

How sweet that song sounds! The boy has a little harp in his hands. Perhaps he is going to play it. Be sure to keep behind the bushes. Do not let him see you!

Listen! He is singing again, and playing on his harp. He looks up at the sky as he sings.

"The heavens declare the glory of God;
And the firmament showeth His handiwork.
Day unto day uttereth speech,
And night unto night showeth knowledge."

What beautiful songs, and how sweetly sung! Who is this boy? How did he learn to play and sing so well?

He has taken up his shepherd's staff. He is going over the hill, calling the sheep. He has a name for each one. The sheep leave their nibbling and run at his call. He is leading them over the hill.

The shepherd has disappeared. We shall often meet him again, however. God has chosen him to play a very important part in the story of His people. This shepherd boy is to become Israel's king.

God had honored Saul by choosing him to be Israel's first king, but Saul had grown proud. He did not care to do what God wanted. He had not obeyed God's commands.

So after a time God told Samuel to fill his horn with oil and to go to Jesse in Bethlehem, for the Lord had chosen one of Jesse's sons to be king instead of Saul.

Samuel went to Bethlehem, calling all the people of the village to a sacrifice. Jesse and his sons came with the others. Only Jesse's youngest son, David, was not called. He stayed in the field, watching the sheep.

Samuel looked at Jesse's oldest son, Eliab, who was very tall and fine looking. He said to himself, "Surely this is the man whom God has chosen to be king."

But God said to Samuel, "Do not judge by his handsome face and his tallness. Man looks on the outward appearance, but God looks into the heart. I have not chosen this one."

Jesse called his next son, Abinadab. Samuel said, "Neither has God chosen this one."

In turn, seven of Jesse's sons came before Samuel. The old prophet said, "God has not chosen any of these. Are these all the sons you have?"

"I have one more, the youngest," Jesse answered. "He is out in the field keeping the sheep."

"Bring him here," Samuel commanded. "We will not sit down to supper till he comes."

David came in from the fields. He was a young boy of sixteen or seventeen. He was tall and fine looking; he had a well-formed body and a fresh, healthy color from being out of doors day after day with the sheep. He was so handsome that people loved to look at him.

When David appeared, God said to Samuel, "Arise and anoint him, for he is the one whom I have chosen to be king."

The prophet called the young boy to him and told him to kneel down. David came, blushing a rosy red, and kneeled before Samuel. The old man took the horn of oil and poured it on David's head.

All David's brothers and the people of Bethlehem saw Samuel do this. From that time on, the Spirit of the Lord came into David's heart. Of course, he did not begin to rule at the moment when he was anointed, for Saul was still living. Saul did not even know that David had been chosen to be king after him. Only at the death of Saul did the kingdom come to David.

Although Saul continued to rule, God was no longer with him. His disobedience had showed that his heart was not good. When God's Spirit left Saul, an evil spirit came to trouble him. At times he was very sad.

Some of Saul's servants said to the king, "Why does not my lord command us to seek out a man who plays well on the harp? When the king feels sad, sweet music will soothe him and make him well again."

"Find me such a man," Saul commanded.

One of the servants said, "I know a man who plays well. He is the son of Jesse, who lives in Bethlehem. He is a brave young man and a good one. He is handsome, too."

At Saul's command David came to the palace to live for a time. When the king had his spells of sickness, David played on his harp. Saul felt better when he heard the lovely songs which David played.

PART 2 — DAVID AND THE GIANT

During all of Saul's reign, there was war with the Philistines. These people lived on the sea coast to the southwest of Judah, in the country where the giants had once lived. They had five big walled cities and many small ones.

Over and over again the Philistines came up to fight with the Israelites. A short time after David had been anointed by Samuel, they again gathered their armies for war. Saul and his soldiers came to meet them. Each army was camped on a mountain, with the valley separating the camps.

With the Philistine army was a man who was more than nine feet tall. His name was Goliath of Gath, and he was one of the few giants left in the land. He could not come into an ordinary house, for he was too tall. He could not squeeze through an ordinary door, for he was too broad. If he could have managed to get in, his head would have hit the ceilings.

This giant was dressed in metal from head to foot. In his hand he held an enormous spear that was so heavy that an ordinary man could not even lift it.

Goliath came out every day and roared a challenge across to the other mountain, where the Israelites stood. He shouted in his fearful voice, "I defy the armies of Israel! Choose a man to fight with me. If he kills me, then we will be your servants. But if I kill him, then you must be our servants."

It was no wonder that the men of Israel were frightened when they saw this giant and heard his boastful words. No one would ever dare to fight with a man so huge. Why, he could kill a hundred men just as easily as he could kill one! No Israelite would dare to answer the giant when he roared his challenge, not even King Saul.

Since Saul was away at war, David had gone home to take care of his father's sheep in the fields of Bethlehem. His older brothers had joined the Israelite army.

One day Jesse, David's father, said to him, "Here are ten loaves of bread and a bushel of parched grain. Take them to your brothers at the camp. Take also these ten cheeses as a present to their captain. Find out how your brothers are getting along."

David left his sheep with a keeper. He got up before daylight so as to get an early start. The soldiers were getting ready to go out to fight as David came to the battlefield. Leaving his presents with a man, he ran quickly into the army to speak with his brothers.

Just as he was talking to them, the terrible giant Goliath came out. He stood on the mountain of the Philistines and shouted again in his fearful voice, "I defy the armies of Israel! Send a man to fight with me!"

All the Israelite soldiers were so scared that they ran in every direction and hid. Some of the soldiers standing near David said, "Did you see that terrible giant? He comes out every day in just that way. King Saul has promised to give a great deal of money to any one who will go and kill the giant. He has even promised to give that man the king's daughter as wife. But in spite of King Saul's promises, no one dares try it. No man would have a chance against such a monster."

David answered, "I will go and fight with this giant. He is only a heathen Philistine. How dare he defy the armies of the living God? God will help us to overcome him."

Some of the soldiers told King Saul what David had said. Saul was so glad to find any one who dared to fight against the giant, that he sent for David. Before Saul, David repeated his offer to face the giant in battle.

"You are not able to go and fight with this giant," King Saul objected. "You are only a boy. He has been a great fighter all his life."

David answered, "While I was keeping my father's sheep, a lion came and took one of my lambs. I ran after the lion and pulled the lamb away from him. When the lion turned to fight me, I caught him by his beard and killed him. At another time, a bear came and took one of my lambs. I killed the bear, too. The Lord kept me safe from the paw of the lion and the paw of the bear. He will also help me to kill this heathen Philistine who has defied the armies of the living God. The Lord will keep him from hurting me."

Seeing that David trusted in God, King Saul said, "Go, then. The Lord be with you!"

At the same time, Saul thought it would be safer for David to wear armor. He put his own helmet of brass on David's head, and a shirt made of little rings of brass on David's body. He also gave David his own sword. But David could hardly walk in this heavy armor. He said to the king, "I cannot wear these things, because I am not used to them."

He put them off again. With his stick in his hand he ran down the mountain side to meet the giant on the other mountain. In the valley between the two mountains ran a little brook. David stopped a moment, picked five smooth stones out of the brook, and put them into a shepherd's bag which he had with him. Holding a sling in his hand, he ran towards the giant.

Goliath, after he had shouted his defiance once again, looked about to see if any man were coming to fight with him. He saw David, but he scorned this boy.

David was actually coming nearer and nearer. The giant called, "Am I a dog, that you are coming to fight me with sticks?"

He began to curse David by his gods, shouting, "Come on, come on! I will give your flesh to the birds of the air to eat, and to the wild beasts."

David shouted back, "You come to me with sword and spear and shield; but I come to you in the name of the Lord of Hosts, the God of the armies of Israel, whom you have defied. Today the Lord will deliver you into my power, so that all the people of the earth shall know that there is a God in Israel. Everybody shall see that the Lord can conquer without sword and spear."

When David said this, Goliath ran forward to kill him. David ran toward the Philistine. He put his hand into his bag and took out a stone, which he put into his sling. He slung the stone right at the giant. The pebble sank down deep into Goliath's forehead. He fell face downward to the ground.

David ran up to the giant. He pulled Goliath's big sword out of the sheath and cut off the giant's enormous head with it.

All the Israelites and Philistines were watching the fight. As soon as the Philistines saw that their giant was dead, they fled as fast as they could go. The men of Israel raised a big shout and ran after them till they came to the gates of the cities of Ekron and Gath.

Many Philistines were killed on this memorable day, and King Saul began to notice this young man who had done so brave a deed.

CHAPTER 69

David Becomes an Outlaw

I Samuel 18, 19, 20

Part 1 — The Cause of the Trouble

Saul was so much pleased with David for killing the giant that he kept the young man at the king's house all the time, and would not let him go home again to his father's house

Saul had a son, named Jonathan, who was just about David's age. The two young men became great friends. Jonathan loved David more than he loved himself, and David loved Jonathan deeply, too. They made a promise always to help each other in time of need.

Since Jonathan was Saul's oldest son, he would become king when his father died. He was always very handsomely dressed, because he was the crown-prince. Jonathan loved David so much that he gave some of his princely clothes to David. He gave David even his sword and his bow and arrows.

David continued living at the king's court. He went wherever King Saul sent him, behaving himself so wisely that Saul made him a captain of the army. Wherever David went, in Saul's house or in the army, people liked him.

But something happened that caused trouble.

When David came back from war with the Philistines, the women of the cities they passed through came out in a procession to meet King Saul. They wanted to show their pleasure in the victories over the Philistines. As they danced joyfully back and forth, shaking their timbrels, some of the women sang, "Saul has slain his thousands." Other women answered in song, "And David his ten thousands."

When Saul heard this singing, he was very angry, and was jealous of David. He grumbled, "They sing that David has slain ten thousands, and that I have slain only thousands. If they think that David is so much better than I am, they will want him to be king instead of me."

The next day, the evil spirit visited Saul. David played on his harp, as he had done before to make Saul feel better after an attack of this sort. Saul had a spear in his hand. His evil thoughts made him hate David. He threw the spear suddenly at David in an attempt to kill him. But David darted out of the way.

The same thing happened a second time.

After this, Saul would no longer have David in his house. He sent him into the army, making him a captain over a thousand soldiers. By this time David had grown to be a man, and the Lord was with him.

When Saul saw how wisely David behaved, he was afraid of him. But all the people of Israel loved him. So Saul thought of another way of killing David. He made up his mind to send David out to war against the Philistines, so that he would be killed in battle. "That will be much better," thought King Saul, "than for me to kill him."

He called David and promised that if he would kill a hundred Philistines, he might have Saul's daughter as wife.

Jonathan was not the only one of Saul's family who loved David. His sister, Michal, was in love with the handsome, brave soldier-musician. David loved Michal in return. To win her he went out very willingly with his thousand soldiers, for he knew that the Lord wanted the Philistines killed.

So David went to war against the Philistines. And they did not kill him, as Saul had hoped. When he returned, Saul gave him the princess Michal as wife. But when Saul saw that his own daughter and all the people loved David, and that the Lord was taking care of him, Saul was the more jealous. He became David's deadly enemy.

Now that this attempt to kill David by sending him against the Philistines had not succeeded, Saul tried another way. He commanded his son Jonathan and his servants to kill David.

Jonathan loved David. Instead of killing him, Jonathan did everything he could to help David and to keep him safe. He told David to hide for a little while until he had a chance to talk with the king. "After that," he said, "I will come and tell you what my father says."

So David did. Jonathan approached Saul, speaking well about David. He said, "Do not hurt David, because he has been very good to you. Do not forget that he risked his life for you when he went and fought against Goliath. You were very glad when he did that. Why should you kill a man who has done nothing but good toward you?"

Saul felt ashamed of himself and he promised that David would not be killed. Jonathan brought David to his father. Once more David lived in Saul's court.

Again the Philistines made war upon the Israelites. David and his thousand soldiers won another splendid victory over the Philistines.

Again Saul became jealous of his handsome young captain. The evil spirit troubled him. One day as he sat in his house listening to David play on his harp, he fell into an ugly temper and again threw his spear at David to kill him. David slipped away, and the spear went into the wall.

This time Saul's fury lasted. He sent messengers to watch David's house and kill him in the morning. Saul's daughter, Michal, defeated her father's plans, for she loved David. She let him down through a window where the messengers could not see him. He escaped to Samuel, who lived in Ramah, and there he stayed for a while.

Part 2 — David and Jonathan

David knew he could not keep on hiding from the king forever. Soon he came back secretly to see his friend Jonathan. He asked him, "What have I done to make your father want to kill me?"

Jonathan said, "You shall not die. I will talk to my father and find out why he is angry with you. He tells me everything, and he will tell me this, too."

"Your father knows that you love me," David replied. "He thinks, 'I will not let Jonathan know that I am going to kill David, because it will make him feel sad.' But truly, Jonathan, there is only a step between me and death."

"What do you want me to do?" Jonathan asked.

"Tomorrow is the time of the new moon," said David. "Your father has always had me eat at his table at the time of the new moon. I shall not come tomorrow.

"If your father asks why I am not there, say, 'David asked me if he might go home to Bethlehem for a few days, because his family has a sacrifice there every year at this time.'

"If your father says, 'That is all right,' then I shall know that it is safe for me to come back. If he is very angry, then I shall know that he surely wants to kill me."

Jonathan said, "If I should know that my father intends to harm you in any way, I would certainly let you know."

"But how will you tell me?" David asked.

Jonathan answered, "Let us go out into the field, where we can talk more freely."

When they were entirely alone in the field, Jonathan said, "To-morrow I will find out how my father feels toward you. If he really intends to kill you, I will surely tell you, so that you can hide from him. I know that God will take care of you and punish all your enemies. The Lord always takes care of those who truly serve Him."

Jonathan loved David so much that he was not jealous, although he knew that God was going to make David king some day. Jonathan was the prince who should have been king after his father, but he knew that God would take the kingdom away from Saul's family and give it to David. All he wished was David's promise that when that time came, he would be kind to Jonathan's children.

"Hide down here in the field for three days," Jonathan told David. "Tomorrow at dinner I will find out what my father intends to do to you. When I come back, I will bring my bows and arrows, as if I were going to practice shooting. I will bring with me a boy to run after my arrows. If I tell him that the arrows are on this side, then you may know that all is safe and that my father intends no harm to you. But if I tell him that the arrows are beyond him, then you may know that my father is not friendly."

The next day was the time of the new moon. Always before, David had sat at the king's table on that day. This time he did not come.

The first day King Saul said nothing. The second day he asked, "Where is David? Why hasn't he come to dinner, yesterday and today?"

Jonathan said, "David begged me to let him go home for a few days, because his family has a sacrifice every year at this time."

Saul flew into a rage. Before all the people at the table he shouted at Jonathan, "You foolish fellow! You are friends with this David to your own hurt. Don't you know that as long as David lives, you will never be king? Go and get him at once, for he shall surely die."

Jonathan protested, "Why do you want to kill him? What harm has he done?"

Saul was in such a temper that he hardly knew what he was doing. He could not speak; he rose from his chair and hurled his spear at Jonathan, his own son.

Jonathan became angry, too. To think that his father should treat David so shamefully! He left the table and would not eat anything. The next morning he went out into the field, taking a boy with him.

As the boy ran, Jonathan shot an arrow beyond him. He called "Look, the arrow is farther on, beyond you." As soon as the boy found the arrow, Jonathan called to him, "Hurry! Hurry!"

Before long, he gave his bow and arrow to the boy, telling him to take them back to the city. When the boy was out of sight, David came out of the place where he had been hiding. Even in this lonely place he had to be very careful not to let anyone see him, for Saul must not discover his hiding place.

David realized now that he would have to go far away, or he would surely be killed. Jonathan knew that he would have to say goodbye to his beloved friend. This was a sad parting. They put their arms around each other and kissed, tears rolling down their cheeks.

Jonathan said, "We will always remember the promise that we have made to each other, for we have sworn in the name of the Lord that we will always be kind to each other's children."

Then with a final "Peace be with you," the two friends went their ways, David into the desert and Jonathan to the palace.

CHAPTER 70

Stories About the Outlawed David

I SAMUEL 21-25

PART 1 — A SERIOUS GAME OF HIDE-AND-SEEK

David knew that he would have to leave the country to escape from Saul. He went down to Gath in the land of the Philistines.

Even there he was not safe, for some men came to their king and said, "Is not this David the king of the Israelites? The women sang of him, 'Saul has slain his thousands, and David his ten thousands.'"

They brought David before the king. But to avoid being captured David pretended to be crazy. He scratched on the doors of the gate and let his spit fall down on his beard. Seeing this, the king said to his servants, "Don't you see that this man is insane? Why do you bring such men here?"

Although David had saved himself this time, he could not stay in that city. Praying to God to help him, he took refuge in a big cave called the cave of Adullam, in the country of Judah. When David's father and brothers heard where he was, they came down there too. It was not safe for them to stay in their own home, for in those times if a king were angry with one man, he tried to kill all his family, too.

A great many Israelites who did not like Saul joined David in the cave. Before long David had four hundred men to follow him.

They could not stay in the cave of Adullam long, for fear Saul would find them. David led his men far away from the land of Israel to a city in the land of Moab, on the other side of the Jordan River. He arranged a safe place in the land of Moab for his father and mother who were too old for the dangers and hardships of his own life. They stayed there during all the time David was hiding from Saul.

Before long, God sent a prophet to David to tell him to return to Judah. David and his four hundred men did as the prophet told them.

And they found a thick wood where they thought they might be safe from Saul.

As soon as Saul heard where David was, he went out with a large army to that place. David and his men had to flee from one place to another to save themselves from Saul. For many days they hid in caves in the rough mountain country. Dangerous as this was, God did not permit the king to find David.

Saul's son, Jonathan, was told that David was hiding in a certain forest. He went to his friend and encouraged him. The two men renewed their solemn promise to each other that their children should be friends forever.

In that country was a certain town whose people were not friendly to David. They offered to help Saul catch the man whom he was hunting. Saul was very much pleased to hear that these men were on his side. He told them to find out just where David was.

In a few days the king went down to that country with his soldiers. Just in time, David heard of Saul's coming. He hurried away as fast as he could, with Saul's army after him.

There seemed to be no chance for David to escape, for his men were almost surrounded by the king's army. When the end seemed very near, a messenger came to Saul and cried, "Make haste, for the Philistines have come into our land!" At the news of this danger, Saul had to give up hunting for David in order to protect the land.

David was saved, but he saw that it would not be safe for him to stay in that place. He went over to a very wild and rough country near the Dead Sea. This place was called En-gedi, or "the rocks of the wild goats." Here David and his men hid in a big cave.

After Saul had driven away the Philistines, he took three thousand of his best soldiers and went to the rocks of the wild goats to hunt for David. He became very tired, and went into a cave to sleep.

Saul had chosen the very cave in which David was hiding, but he did not see David and his men who were in the darkness at the back of the cave. Without bothering to look around at all, he lay down and went to sleep.

David's men whispered softly, "At last God has given you a chance to kill your enemy." Without answering a word, David walked quietly to the place where Saul lay. With his sword he cut off a part of the king's loose, flowing robe; but he would not let his soldiers touch the king.

After Saul had slept for some time, he awoke and went out of the cave. David went to the opening and called after him, "My lord the king!"

Saul turned around to see who was calling him. Whom should he see but David, the very man he was hunting!

David bowed himself down to the earth and said, "Why do you believe those who say I am your enemy? This very day I could have killed you, for God gave you into my power. But I said, 'I will not kill him, for God anointed him to be king.' See, my father, I could easily have killed you, but I only cut off a piece of your robe. Why do you try to kill me? The Lord will punish you if you harm me, but I will never try to kill you."

Saul was startled to see David. When he heard these friendly words and saw that David had saved his life, he felt very much ashamed.

He called back, "Is this your voice, my son David?" He was so sorry that he had been cruel to David that tears rolled down his cheeks. He continued, "You have been good, but I have been bad. I wanted to kill you, but you have saved my life. God will reward you for what you have done today. I know that you will be king some day. Promise me that you will not kill my children when that day comes."

David made this promise to Saul before the king went home. David and his men went back to the cave, however, for Saul could not be trusted. At any moment his ugly temper might come upon him, and then he might again suddenly try to kill David.

PART 2 — A WISE WIFE AND A FOOLISH HUSBAND

At this time the good old prophet Samuel died. All the people of Israel went to Ramah to his funeral. David could not go, for he could not trust Saul. Neither did he dare to stay in his cave, since Saul had found that hiding place.

With his men David went south of the Dead Sea to the Wilderness of Paran, another rough country. On his way he had to pass by the farm of a very rich man named Nabal. This man was cross and stingy, but he had a very charming wife who was as sensible and generous as she was beautiful.

It was the time of year when the sheep were sheared. Since Nabal had many sheep and goats, he hired some men to come and shear the animals. He made a feast for these men, preparing a great deal of food.

David often had a hard time to get enough food for himself and his followers; for he now had over six hundred men with him in the wilderness. When he heard that the sheep-shearers were Nabal's servants, he sent ten young men to Nabal with this message:

"I have heard that the sheep-shearers belong to you. All the time that your shepherds were with us, we did not hurt them. We never took away any of their sheep. Now, I pray you, be generous and give us a little of the food that you have prepared for your servants."

In those days it was considered very rude to turn away any one who asked hospitality. But the stingy Nabal answered, "And who is David? Nowadays there are many servants who run away from their masters. Does he want me to take him some of the bread and meat and water that I have prepared for my shearers, and give them to men who are strangers to me? I shall do no such thing."

The young men went back to David and told him how rudely Nabal had answered them. David was so angry that he told his men to get ready to go and punish Nabal.

In the meantime, one of Nabal's servants had heard that David was coming to punish his master. The young man quickly ran to Nabal's wife, Abigail, and said to her, "David sent messengers to speak to our master, but he flew into a rage at them. David's men were very good to our shepherds while they were in the fields keeping the sheep. They protected our men from thieves and from wild beasts. But now David is angry at the way our master has spoken to the young men whom he sent, and he is coming here to punish us. You must decide quickly what to do to stop him, or he will come here and do us harm. We cannot even speak to our master."

Abigail was as wise as she was beautiful. She acted quickly. She took two hundred loaves of bread, two big wine-skins full of wine, five sheep already cooked, five measures of parched wheat like popcorn, a hundred clusters of raisins, and two hundred cakes of figs. She loaded these provisions on the backs of asses and sent some servants to David with them. She herself rode on another ass and followed them. She did not tell her husband, Nabal, what she had done and what she was going to do.

As soon as Abigail saw David, she slipped from the back of the ass. Bowing down to the ground very politely, she apologized for the way her husband had acted.

Then she said, "I know that one day the Lord will make you victorious over all your enemies, and will make you ruler over all Israel. Then you will be glad that you have not killed any of Nabal's family."

David was very much pleased with this beautiful and gracious woman. He answered, "Blessed be the Lord God of Israel who sent you to meet me today. Blessed be your good advice, which has kept me from coming to kill Nabal. If you had not come, I would surely have punished him and his family tonight."

Abigail went home. Nabal was having a feast in his house, a feast rich enough for a king. He was very drunk. Abigail told him nothing of what she had done. In the morning, when he was no longer drunk, she told him about the danger he had been in, and how David and his men had been coming to kill him. Nabal was so frightened that his heart almost stopped beating. About ten days after that God sent a sickness to Nabal, and he died.

When David heard of Nabal's death, he sent some messengers to Abigail to ask her to become his wife. So Abigail mounted her ass again and went to live with David.

CHAPTER 71

More Stories About David and Saul

I SAMUEL 26, 30, 31;   II SAMUEL 1

PART 1 — DAVID SAVES HIS ENEMY

Saul did not keep his promise not to try to harm David. He might have done so, if it had not been for the people who lived near the place where David was hiding. These people were not friendly to David, and they told the king where he was.

So Saul went to hunt for David in the wilderness with an army of three thousand soldiers. David's spies soon brought the news that the king was again hunting for him.

One night David and one of his soldiers went to the place where Saul and his men lay sleeping. God sent a sound sleep upon Saul's soldiers. None of them awakened when David and his comrade stole softly into the camp. King Saul, too, was fast asleep. His spear was stuck into the ground at his head, with a pitcher of water close by. His general, Abner, was sleeping close to the king.

David's companion spoke softly to him. "God has given you this chance to kill your enemy. Let me kill him with one stroke of my spear. I won't have to strike him a second time."

David again refused. "No," he said. "God has anointed Saul to be king. I will not kill the Lord's anointed one. Some day he will fall in battle, or his time will come to die peacefully, but I will not kill him."

Taking Saul's spear and pitcher of water with them, David and Abishai made their way to the top of a hill some distance away. David then called to Saul's general. "Abner, Abner, do you hear me? I thought you were the bravest of the king's soldiers. If you are so brave, why haven't you taken care of your master, the king? Some one came near to kill the king, Abner! You have not taken care of him as you should! Where is the king's spear, and the bottle of water that was by his head?"

When King Saul heard David, he called, "Is this your voice, my son David?"

David answered, "It is my voice, my lord, O king! Why did you come here after me? You have driven me out of the Lord's country into a heathen land. Why do you hunt for one so unimportant as I am?"

Saul realized he was guilty. "I have done wrong," he cried. "Come back, my son David, for I will not again try to harm you, because you have not killed me tonight, when you had a chance."

David answered, "Here is your spear. Let one of the young men come over and get it. As I have saved your life today, so may the Lord save my life, and deliver me from all my troubles."

When Saul saw what a noble soul David had, he exclaimed, "Blessed are you, my son David! You will do great things."

Although Saul went home without trying to harm David, he could not be trusted. He had already broken his promise once. David said to himself, "Saul will surely kill me some day if I stay here in the country of the Israelites. The best thing for me is to escape into the country of the Philistines. When Saul hears that I have left the country, he will stop hunting for me."

David took his six hundred men, with their wives and their children and all that they had, over the boundary into the land of the Philistines.

The king of this country was very friendly. When David asked him, the king gave him the town of Ziklag, in the desert to the south. Here David was joined by more Israelites. Many people sympathized with him in his struggle with Saul. They knew he had done nothing against the king. Probably, too, some of them had heard that Samuel had anointed David to be king in the presence of the people of Bethlehem.

Some of the best soldiers of the Israelites agreed to go down to help David. These were brave men. They were so skillful with bow and arrow that they could shoot with the left hand as well as with the right. They handled a shield nimbly. They could run as fast as wild deer.

David made these men captains of his band. For a year and four months they all lived in Ziklag.

PART 2 — THE DEATH OF SAUL

After some time, the Philistines made ready for another big battle with the Israelites. David was still living among the Philistines; so he and his men went to Gath, the royal city of the Philistines, to go with them against the Israelites.

But the lords of the Philistines did not want to take David and his men with them — they were afraid David would turn against them in battle. They remembered that women had sung, "Saul slew his thousands and David his ten thousands."

It was certainly well that the Philistines did not let David join them, for two reasons. The first reason is that a sad thing happened in that battle, and David would never have forgiven himself if he had had a part in it. The second reason is that when David returned to Ziklag he found the city burned. Wandering Amalekites had burned the city and run off with all the women and children.

When David and his men saw their homes burned and knew their wives and children had been stolen away, they cried until they could cry no more. David asked the Lord if he should pursue the Amalekites.

God told him to go after them, promising that he would recover all that had been stolen.

David and four hundred of his men started after the Amalekites. They did not know which way the thieves had gone, for there was no one living in that wild, lonely country.

In a field they found a poor sick man who had been left behind by the Amalekites. He was almost dead of starvation, for he had had nothing to eat or drink for three days and nights. Lifting him up, the Israelites gave him some bread and water, with some dried figs and raisins.

After the man had eaten, he revived enough to speak. They asked him if he knew where the Amalekites had gone. He said, "Yes, I will show you the way, if you will promise not to kill me."

In their camp the Amalekites were eating and drinking and dancing, because they had taken so much treasure out of the land of the Philistines and out of the land of Judah. David attacked them at once. They fought all night and until the evening of the next day. All the Amalekites were killed, except four hundred young men, who galloped swiftly away on camels.

David's men got back everything that had been stolen — all their wives and sons and daughters, and all the flocks and herds. Besides that, they took all the cattle belonging to the Amalekites who had been killed.

Meanwhile the Philistines had prepared for war and marched far into the country of the Israelites. There was a great battle in the mountain of Gilboa, about two hundred miles north of the place where David was.

The Philistines fought hard. They gained the victory over the Israelites. Many of the Israelites were killed or very severely wounded by the arrows of the Philistines.

Jonathan and two other sons of Saul were killed. And the soldiers followed hard after Saul. He was afraid that if the Philistines should capture him, they would torture him. He said to the man who carried his armor, "Draw your sword and thrust it through me, so that I may die."

The armor-bearer would not kill Saul, for he was afraid to do so dreadful a thing. Saul took his own sword and stuck it in the ground, with the point up. Then he fell upon his sword to kill himself. He did not die at once, however. While he was in great pain, he saw a young man, an Amalekite. The wounded king managed to say, "Please kill me, for I am suffering dreadfully."

The young man saw that, although the sword had not gone deep enough to kill Saul quickly, he could not live. He did as Saul asked. When Saul was dead, the young man took the crown from his head and the bracelet from his arm, and carried them away.

The day after the battle, the Philistines came to the battlefield to strip the dead and to steal any treasures that they had. They found the bodies of Saul's three sons. When they found Saul's body, they were very glad. They sent the news of Saul's death into all parts of their land. His armor they put into one of their temples.

Most shocking of all, they fastened Saul's body and the bodies of his three sons on the wall of one of their towns, to insult the people whose king Saul had been. That night, some brave Israelites came and took down the bodies of Saul and his sons and buried them under a tree. The Israelites mourned for seven days after the battle.

All this time, David knew nothing of what had been going on. He and his men were far away in the desert, fighting the wild Amalekites.

Two days after David and his soldiers had conquered the Amalekites and had brought back their wives and children to Ziklag, a young man came to their town. His clothes were torn and he had earth upon his head.

People saw that he was the bearer of news and gathered around him. "Where have you come from?" asked David.

The young man answered, "I have escaped out of the camps of Israel."

Of course, David and his followers listened eagerly. David asked, "Tell me how the battle went."

The young man said, "The Philistines have conquered, and many Israelites have been killed. Saul and his son Jonathan are dead also."

This was very important news, for it meant that David could now be king. "How do you know that Saul is dead?" David asked.

The young man told how he helped Saul die. He gave David Saul's crown and bracelet. When David heard all this, he tore his clothes and his soldiers did the same. They mourned and fasted until the evening, in memory of Saul and Jonathan, and for all the Israelite soldiers who had died.

CHAPTER 72

David, the King Whom God Loved

II SAMUEL 2, 5-10

PART 1 — THE ARK IS BROUGHT BACK

Now that Saul and his sons were dead, the children of Israel were without a king. David knew that he was to rule after Saul's death, because Samuel had anointed him.

He asked the Lord where he should go to be proclaimed king. The Lord told him to go up to Hebron. Therefore David and his men left the burned city of Ziklag to live in the country around Hebron.

The death of Saul and his sons did not make the Israelites sad for a long time. The people knew that David would become their king, and they loved him.

Great numbers of soldiers made ready to go to Hebron to crown their new king. Day by day they poured into the city, until there was a great host of nearly three hundred thousand men who had come to show their loyalty to David.

And so amid great joy and rejoicing David was crowned. He was thirty years old when he became king, and he reigned for forty years. The first seven happy years were spent in Hebron, where he had been crowned. Afterwards, Jerusalem became the royal city. It was built on a high hill, with deep valleys on three sides. It would be easy to defend in case of war.

After David and his leaders went to live in Jerusalem, the city was often called "The city of David." The king built a splendid palace with fine cedar trees sent by Hiram, king of Tyre. He built other fine houses in Jerusalem, making it a beautiful city.

David became a great king, for God was with him. David loved the Lord and tried always to serve Him.

Some time after David had been living in Jerusalem, he remembered that the golden Ark of the Lord was still in Kirjath-jearim. It had been there for twenty years, ever since it had been captured and returned by the Philistines.

King David talked with all the important men of the country, suggesting that they bring the Ark to Jerusalem, the royal city. The people were very much pleased to hear this suggestion.

All the people went together to Kirjath-jearim. They put the Ark upon a new cart which was driven by two men. The people walked beside the cart while David played on his harp. As they went along, some of the people played on cymbals, on psalteries, on cornets, and on timbrels, so that beautiful music accompanied the Ark.

In one place the road was very rough, and the oxen which were drawing the cart stumbled. Uzza, one of the men driving the oxen, put out his hand to steady the Ark. But God did not wish His holy Ark to be touched by profane hands. Uzza fell down dead, without time to cry out.

This happening frightened David and the people. Without going any farther, they carried the Ark into a house near by. There it stayed for three months. Then, because God blessed the house greatly in that time, David finally gathered courage to bring the Ark to Jerusalem.

This time the Levites carried the Ark upon their shoulders, as Moses had commanded. Once more David and all the people danced and sang as they went along. With music and dancing and rejoicing the Ark was brought to Jerusalem, where a tent had been made ready to receive it.

Sacrifices were offered to the Lord. David appointed some of the Levites to take care of the Ark. He blessed all the people, giving every one a loaf of bread and a big piece of meat and a cake of raisins.

The people praised God with music as well as with sacrifices. Their king was a skilled player on the harp, and many of the other Israelites were fine musicians. David called together a great many singers and players and divided them into choirs. He also wrote a long song which was recited before the Ark of the Covenant. This song ended,

> "Blessed be Jehovah, the God of Israel,
> From everlasting even to everlasting."

And all the people said "Amen," and praised the Lord.

Once more worship was centered around the Ark. David became a great king, for God was with him.

One day David realized that while he was living in a fine house, God's holy Ark was sheltered only by a tent. A beautiful thought came into his heart. He planned to make a grand temple for God's house, covered with gold and splendidly decorated. The prophet Nathan was pleased with David's plan.

That night God spoke to Nathan and gave him a message for David. Since He had brought the children of Israel out of the land of Egypt, God had not commanded that a temple be built.

God had taken David from his sheep and had made him a king over Israel. God would give him children who would be kings after him, and He would be with David's children forever. But the temple must not be built by a man whose life had been filled with war, as David's life had been. His son, who would be king after him, would build God's house.

David felt very thankful and humble when he had heard God's promise that his children should be kings over Israel forever. He gave up his plan of building a temple, but he made things ready for his son to build it.

PART 2 — A FRIENDLY MESSAGE WHICH BROUGHT WAR

King David had many wars. God gave him victories over his enemies, the Philistines. It was customary for these people to carry their idols into battle with them, for they thought that these gods could help them with the battle. In the battle with David, however, they were so badly beaten that they fled, leaving their idols to be burned by the Israelites.

The Israelites also made servants of the Moabites, who lived on the east side of the Jordan River.

Then David went into the north, far beyond where the Israelites lived. He conquered the northern land as far as the Euphrates River on the east. All the people of this northern land became subject to King David. Long before, God had promised to give to Israel all the land from the Euphrates River to the river of Egypt, but until David's time the Israelites had not been able to overcome these countries.

David took great quantities of silver and gold from all the countries where he had been fighting. He brought all this silver and gold and brass to Jerusalem, saving it up for the beautiful temple which God had said his son should make.

After David had conquered the northern people, he fought against the Edomites, who lived south of the Dead Sea. David sent one of his generals to lead in battle. Many of the Edomites were killed, and David became ruler over this southern country, too.

Do you remember that cruel King Nahash of Ammon, who had threatened to put out the right eyes of the men of Jabesh-gilead, when Saul began to reign? He died, and his son, Hanun, began to rule. David politely sent some messengers to King Hanun, to comfort him at the death of his father.

But the servants of Hanun said to their king, "Do not think that King David has sent these messengers to comfort you because of the death of your father. No, indeed; it is much more likely that he sent them to spy out the land."

When King Hanun heard his servants speak in this way, he did a very shameful thing to David's messengers. King Hanun took David's men, and shaved off one-half of their beards, and cut off half of their clothes.

Some one hurried to tell King David in what a shameful and insulting way his messengers had been treated.

David immediately sent word to the men to stay at Jericho until their beards were grown, for they were greatly ashamed, since every man in those days wore a long beard. Jericho had not been built up again since Joshua had conquered it and burned it to the ground. At this time no one lived there but a few country people, so that the men could stay there without being seen until their beards were grown.

David was very angry to have his messengers, whom he had sent in kindness, treated so insultingly. He sent his finest soldiers, under his general Joab, into the country of Ammon to fight Hanun. He himself stayed at Jerusalem.

Hanun saw that there would be a big battle. He sent for help to the king of the Syrians whom David had beaten before. They sent to other kings beyond the Euphrates River.

Joab sent word to David, asking him to come and help. With many more soldiers, David joined Joab. Together they fought against the large army of the enemy.   Since God helped the brave Israelites, the other nations were beaten and became the servants of King David. They did not dare to join again to make war upon the Israelites.

David was now a very great king.   He had conquered the Ammonites to the east of the Jordan and the Syrians as far north as the Euphrates River, and the Edomites to the south, in Mount Seir.   All these nations became David's servants.

Now that his kingdom was established safely, David tried to find out if there were any of Saul's children or grandchildren to whom he could show kindness.   He heard that one of Saul's old servants, Ziba, was still living.   King David sent for Ziba and asked him, "Are there any of Saul's family left? I should like to be kind to them."

Ziba answered, "There is a son of Jonathan, named Mephibosheth. He is lame.   He was five years old when that terrible battle was fought between the Israelites and the Philistines, in which his father, Jonathan, and his grandfather, Saul, were killed.   When the news of the battle came, his nurse took him up in a hurry to hide him.   In her haste, she dropped the little boy.   He has been lame in both his feet ever since."

The king said, "Find him for me and bring him here."

When Mephibosheth came to the king, David remembered his love for Jonathan and the sacred promise he had made to him.   He said tenderly, "Mephibosheth."

The man bowed down to the ground and answered rather tremblingly, "I am your servant," for he did not know what the king wanted of him.

David said, "Do not be afraid, Mephibosheth. I will surely be kind to you, for the sake of your father, Jonathan. I will give back to you all the land which belonged to your grandfather, Saul. You yourself shall eat at my table with my own sons."

King David gave back to Mephibosheth all the land that had belonged to Saul.   Ziba farmed the land for him.   Jonathan's lame son lived in Jerusalem and ate at the king's table.

So David remembered his promise to his friend.

CHAPTER 73

How the Good King Sinned

II SAMUEL 11, 12

One evening when David could not sleep very well, he got up out of bed and went up to the roof of his house. Perhaps it was cooler there; or perhaps David enjoyed the bright moonlight. All the roofs in Canaan were flat, with a railing around them. People often sat on their roofs, or slept there.

David could see down into the court of a near-by house where a woman was washing herself. She was very beautiful. David sent one of his servants to ask the woman to come to see him.

This woman was Bathsheba, the wife of a man called Uriah, who had gone to war for David. Bathsheba came to see David, and the king fell in love with her. He could not have her for his wife, because she was already married. David gave himself over to wicked thoughts. "Oh, if only her husband should be killed in the war! Then I could marry her."

David wanted her so much that he sent a letter to his general, Joab, telling him to put Uriah in the front of the hottest battle, so that he might die.

Joab did this. He put Uriah at a most dangerous position near the wall of the city. Some archers on the top of the city wall shot Uriah. He died, as David had hoped.

When Bathsheba, the wife of Uriah, heard that her husband was dead, she mourned for him. After a time, David married her. Before long a little son was born to them.

What David had done displeased the Lord. He sent the prophet, Nathan, to David. Nathan told David this story:

"There were two men in one city. One was rich; the other was poor. The rich man had a great many flocks and herds, but the poor man had only one little lamb, which he had brought up and fed. It ate from his plate, and drank from his own cup, and slept in his bed with him. He loved it as much as if it had been his daughter.

"A traveler happened to visit the rich man. Instead of taking one of his own sheep to make a nice dinner for the traveler, the rich man took the poor man's lamb, and killed it."

When David heard this story, he became very angry. "As the Lord lives," he exclaimed, "the man who has done this shall surely die. He shall give four lambs back to the poor man."

The prophet Nathan said, *"Thou* art the man! The Lord says, 'I anointed you king over Israel. I saved you from Saul, giving you the kingdom. You have many wives. Why have you done this wicked thing? Uriah had only one wife. You have killed him with the sword of the Ammonites, and have taken his wife to be your wife. I will certainly punish you for this.' "

David realized how sinful he had been. He was very, very sorry.

Nathan said, "The Lord will forgive you if you repent. You shall not die, but because you have done this wicked thing, the baby shall surely die."

With these words Nathan went away. As he had said, the baby soon became very sick. David loved the child very much. He knew the baby was dying because he had sinned. He could not bear to look at its dear little face, hot with fever.

He lay down on the ground all night, and prayed to God to save the child's life. The men of his house went in to raise him up from the ground, but he would not rise nor eat with them.

After seven days, the baby died. David's servants were afraid to tell him that the child was dead. They whispered to one another, "While the child was still alive he would not listen to us. How much more will he grieve now that the child is dead!"

When David saw his servants whispering, he asked them, "Is the child dead?"

"He is dead," they said.

David arose from the ground and washed himself and put on clean clothes. He went first of all to the house of the Lord to worship. Then he went to his own house and ate some food.

His servants were surprised. "How is this?" they asked. "When the child was still alive you fasted and wept; and now he is dead you arise and eat."

David answered, "While the child was still alive I fasted and wept, for I said, 'Perhaps God will be gracious to me and will let the child live.' But now he is dead, why should I fast? I cannot bring him back again. I shall go to him, but he will not return to me."

The next year, God gave David and Bathsheba another baby. They named him Solomon. God loved Solomon.

In his sorrow for his sin, David wrote a beautiful song—the fifty-first psalm.

"Purify me with hyssop, and I shall be clean:
Wash me, and I shall be whiter than snow.
O Lord, open Thou my lips,
And my mouth shall show forth Thy praise.
For Thou delightest not in sacrifice; else would I give it.
Thou hast no pleasure in burnt-offering.
The sacrifices of God are a broken spirit.
A broken and a contrite heart, O God, Thou wilt not despise."

CHAPTER 74

The Plan of a Bad Son

II SAMUEL 21: 15, 16; I CHRONICLES 20

PART 1 — THE PRINCE WHO WANTED TO BE KING

Do you remember how David had killed the giant Goliath with a stone? Three of Goliath's sons were still living in the country of the Philistines to the west of the land of the Israelites. These three men were giants, as their father had been. One of them had six fingers on each hand, and six toes on each foot. Like their father, they fought against the Israelites; and like Goliath, they were killed.

Except for this fighting, King David had peace for a long time. His oldest sons were grown men, while little Solomon was still a child. David's third son, Absalom, was a very handsome man, and David loved him especially.

In all the land there was not another young man so good-looking as Absalom. He had wonderful hair, which hung long and heavy over his shoulders. It was so thick that at the end of each year the part that was cut off weighed six pounds.

Naturally the people talked about the king's son. Absalom liked to be noticed. He was married and lived in a house of his own. He liked to put on a great deal of style.

When Absalom went anywhere, he had a fine chariot to ride in, and fifty men to run before him. When the people saw this procession coming down the streets of Jerusalem, they would stop in admiration and say. "There comes the king's son, Absalom. How beautiful he is!"

They did not know that he was not as good as he was handsome.

Absalom tried hard to make the people of Israel love him. He stood in the gate of the city. If some man from the country came to Jerusalem to settle some dispute he had had with a neighbor, Absalom called to him and asked him what was the trouble. The man would be glad to have the king's son listen to his story.

Absalom would be very friendly to the man. Instead of letting the man bow to him, he would put his arm around the man and kiss him.

In itself, of course, this was all right. It was good to be kind and friendly. But Absalom did not do these things because he was really friendly to the people, but because he wanted to be king some day. He thought that if he could win the love of the people, they would later help him to become king, even though he was not chosen by his father.

And so he would say to the man with whom he talked, "See, your matter is right, but the king has no time to hear you. If I were made judge in the land, I would do justice to every man."

The man would go away thinking, "What a fine man the king's son Absalom is! What a fine king he would make!"

Absalom did this for a long, long time. He became acquainted with many of the country people who came up to Jerusalem to be judged. They all went away with a very friendly feeling for Absalom in their hearts. "So Absalom stole the hearts of the men of Israel."

Meanwhile, King David was reigning in peace and comfort. He had a long and happy rule. He had conquered his enemies and extended his kingdom to the north and south and east. The people in these conquered countries were his servants. David was feared and honored in all lands.

Most important of all, David truly worshipped God. In his time, the children of Israel served God and put away all their idols. David organized a choir of many singers for the Tabernacle to praise God. He built up Jerusalem into a strong and splendid city, of which the Hebrews were very proud. The land was prosperous and happy in David's reign. All the people loved their good king.

But this peace did not last. When David was getting to be an old man, his son Absalom made trouble for him.

Ever since the birth of Solomon, David had intended him to be king. From the time that he was a little child, Solomon showed the promise of a wise and beautiful character. The Lord loved Solomon, for he was more like his father David than the other sons were.

Perhaps Absalom knew that King David planned to have Solomon become king after he was dead. If so, he did not intend to pay any attention to his father's wishes. He made up his mind that he himself was going to become king.

PART 2 — KING DAVID RUNS AWAY

Absalom's character was so mean and deceitful, that he did not have even the grace to wait until his father was dead before he started trouble. One day he asked his father if he might go down to the city of Hebron to keep a vow.

Absalom had been planning for years to seize the kingdom. All his plans had been made beforehand. He had sent spies throughout the whole kingdom, telling them as soon as they heard the sound of trumpets, to shout out to the people, "Absalom is king in Hebron!"

With him Absalom took two hundred men from Jerusalem. He also sent for David's wise man, Ahithophel, to come and counsel him.

At that time there was no telegraph or telephone to send news flying here and there. It might be two or three days before King David would hear of what Absalom was doing. Absalom would have plenty of time to collect a big army.

For many years Absalom had been stealing the hearts of the men of Israel by pretending to be friendly to them. So when they heard the spies proclaiming, "Absalom is king in Hebron," many of them flocked to his side.

Someone who was still loyal to David ran to Jerusalem with the news that all the people of Israel had gone over to his son.

The news came as a great shock to David as he sat quietly in his house. He loved Absalom, but he knew that his son was a dangerous man; for Absalom in a fit of anger had killed his oldest brother, Amnon.

But David had not dreamed that Absalom might fight against his own father. He was not prepared for war. He did not know how large an army his son might have.

He said to his servants, "Let us hurry to get away, for Absalom may come with a big army and fight against the city and kill all the people."

So King David and all his household left Jerusalem in a hurry. He did not go alone, for those six hundred brave men who had been with him while he had to defend himself against Saul went with him. The Levites went too, carrying the Ark.

David said to Zadok and Abiathar, the priests, "Do not come with me, but go back into the city with the Ark of God. If God is pleased with me, He will bring me back again some day. Stay in the city with your sons, Ahimaaz and Jonathan. You are priests, and Absalom will not hurt you. You must find out for me what is going on, and send me word by your sons."

David and all the people who were with him went over the brook Kidron and up the side of Mount Olivet.

David felt very sad to think that his own son, whom he loved so much, had conspired against him. Poor David's heart was almost broken. He felt very humble, because he knew that God was sending this trouble upon him as a punishment for killing Uriah. Bare-foot, his head covered, David went up the Mount of Olives, crying as he went. All those with him covered their heads, weeping with David.

Some one announced to David, "Ahithophel, your wise counselor, has gone over to Absalom!" This was a dreadful blow to David. He prayed to God, "O Lord, I pray Thee, turn the counsel of Ahithophel into foolishness."

As David came to the top of Mount Olivet, David's other counselor, Hushai, came to meet him. His coat was torn, and he had put earth upon his head.

David was very glad to see that Hushai was friendly to him. He said, "Go back to the city, Hushai. Go back to Absalom and say to him, 'I will be your servant, O king, as I have been your father's servant till now.' In that way, you may fool Absalom and work against Ahithophel. The priests are in Jerusalem, and they have their sons with them. As soon as you have any news, you can send it to me by those two young men."

So Hushai returned to Jerusalem.

David and his men went on past Mount Olivet. They were met by Ziba, the head servant of the household of Mephibosheth. With him were a few asses loaded with bread, raisins, fruits, and a bottle made of skin and filled with wine.

The king said to Ziba, "What are these?"

Ziba answered, "The asses are for the king's family to ride on, and the bread and fruits are for the people to eat, and the wine is for anyone who feels faint for a drink."

"Where is your master, Mephibosheth?" asked David.

Ziba told a wicked lie. "He is staying in Jerusalem, for he says 'Today the people will make me king, and give back to me the kingdom of my father, Saul.'"

David said, "If that is so, I will give to you all the land which was Saul's, which I gave before to Mephibosheth."

The deceitful Ziba thanked the king.

After King David had gone a little farther, there came out a man who was related to King Saul. This man, Shimei, threw stones at David and cursed him, saying, "You wicked, cruel man! You are being punished now for taking Saul's kingdom away. The Lord is giving the kingdom to your son, because you are a blood-thirsty man."

Abishai, one of David's generals, felt angry. "Why should this dead dog curse my lord the king? Let me go over, I pray you, and cut off his head."

David was so sad to think that his own son was rebelling against him, that he answered Abishai, "Let him curse. The Lord has said to him, 'Curse David.' If my own son has turned against me and is trying to kill me, how much more may this man do it!"

And so King David ran away from the son whom he loved.

CHAPTER 75

The Failure of the Plot

II SAMUEL 17-19

PART 1 — GOOD ADVICE AND BAD

While King David was fleeing from Jerusalem, Absalom and many of the people of Israel came to the city. David's wise counselor, Ahithophel, was with them.

The other wise man, Hushai, was still faithful to David, but he knew that he could help David best by giving Absalom bad advice. He came to Absalom and said, "Long live the king! Long live the king!"

Absalom was surprised. "Is this your kindness to your friend David? Why didn't you go with him?"

Hushai said, "If the Lord and all the people of Israel choose you to be king, then I will stay with you. Why shouldn't I serve the son faithfully, just as I have served the father?"

Hushai seemed to be very much in earnest. Absalom was satisfied, accepting him as second counselor. Then the new king asked Ahithophel, "Now, what do you advise me to do?"

Ahithophel was so wise that he seemed to speak from God. He said, "Let me choose out twelve thousand men and go after David. I will come upon him while he is tired and weak. The people who are with him will run away, and I will kill only the king. All the people I will bring to you, and you shall be king in peace."

Absalom was greatly pleased with this wise advice. He would not follow it, however, until he had first heard what Hushai had to say.

Hushai very well knew that Ahithophel's counsel was wise, and he did not want Absalom to follow it. He said, therefore:

The people ran along beside the king's procession. 2 Samuel 19

"Send me cedar trees out of the mountains of Lebanon." ɪ Kings 5

"The counsel that Ahithophel has given is not good at this time. Your father and the men who are with him are mighty men. They are angry now, like a bear robbed of her cubs. Your father will be too wise to stay with the people tonight. He will hide in some cave, or in some other secret place. If we go up there tonight and some of our soldiers are killed, then our people will be frightened and will run away.

"Instead of going tonight, it will be better for you to wait till you can gather the whole nation of Israel and fight an open battle with your father. If you do this, we shall be so many that we can easily overcome him. Not one of his soldiers will be left. If he has got into a walled city, then we will pull down the walls till not one stone is left."

When Absalom and his friends heard this advice, they thought the counsel of Hushai better than the counsel of Ahithophel. It really was worse, but God made Absalom prefer Hushai's bad advice, in order to bring evil upon Absalom.

Ahithophel's feelings were very much hurt, when Hushai's advice was taken instead of his. He left Jerusalem and went back home to his own town. There he hanged himself and died, leaving only David's friend Hushai to advise Absalom.

Hushai let no time go by before he went to Zadok and Abiathar, the priests. He told them first the counsel which the other wise man had given to Absalom, and then his own advice. He said to them, "Send your sons quickly to David, and tell him it will not be safe for him to stay tonight on this side of the Jordan River. He must hasten to cross the river to the other side."

Jonathan and Ahimaaz, the sons of the priests, had not dared to come into Jerusalem, but were staying outside in the country by a spring. A young girl went out and gave them the message. They were seen by someone, who went and told Absalom that he had seen some men who seemed to be spies. Absalom sent some servants after Jonathan and Ahimaaz.

In the meantime, the two young men had come to a house which had a well. They slid down into the well and hid. The woman of the house spread a cloth over the mouth of the well, scattering ground corn on the cloth.

Soon Absalom's servants came past. They asked, "Where are Jonathan and Ahimaaz?"

The woman answered, "They have gone over the brook."

The servants went on and looked for the young men. They returned to the city without having found any trace of them.

As soon as they were sure it was safe, Jonathan and Ahimaaz climbed out of the well and ran to David. They told him he had better cross the river at once. Absalom had decided to follow Hushai's advice, and gather a big army; but he might at any time change his mind, and start out after David without waiting.

All night long David and his men crossed the Jordan River. By early morning they were all on the other side.

They went on towards a city which was far away from Jerusalem. Here David was given a fine present of food for his people. Besides this, he was given kettles to cook in, and dishes to eat from, and heavy rugs, such as the people in that country use to sleep on.

Some of these things were given by the son of the king who had once threatened to put out the eyes of the men of Jabesh-gilead. Part were brought by a very old man named Barzillai.

Many of the people of Israel still loved David and sympathized with him. As he passed through the country, the people came out of their houses. They wept to think that their good king should be so ill-treated by his own son. Many of the men left their farms and joined David's company, so as to be able to fight for their king if there should be a battle with Absalom's soldiers.

Soon David had a large army. There were thousands of soldiers with him, ready and eager to fight for their king. David divided his soldiers into three parts. He set his general Joab over one-third of the soldiers; and Joab's brother, Abishai, over another third; and a man called Ittai, over the other third.

David promised, "I will go out with you to battle."

But the people said, "No, you must not go. If we run away, they will not care for us; and if half of us die, they will not care. But you are worth ten thousand of us. Stay in the city, ready to help."

PART 2 — ABSALOM'S DEATH

Absalom followed Hushai's advice. He came over the River Jordan with a big army, and was getting ready for a great battle in a large forest that was near the city where David was.

David's army went out of the city to meet Absalom's soldiers. David stood in the gate as his thousands of soldiers marched out. He spoke a special word to his three generals: "Deal gently for my sake with the young man Absalom." He loved Absalom so much that he did not want him harmed, even though he was wicked.

The two armies met in the wood. Absalom's army was beaten. Twenty thousand men were killed. To get away from David's soldiers, Absalom urged his mule into a gallop. As he sped forward under a thick oak tree, his head was caught in the low branches of the tree. Absalom was hung up between heaven and earth, his long hair tangled in the tree, and the mule went on from under him.

A young man saw this happen, and ran to Joab, exclaiming, "I saw Absalom hanging in an oak tree!"

Joab was a stern soldier, a man of iron. He did not intend to deal gently with the prince, for he thought Absalom deserved to die. "Why did you not kill him?" he asked. "I would have given you ten shekels of silver and a girdle."

But the young man answered, "If you had given me a thousand shekels of silver, I would not have put forth my hand to kill the king's son! I myself heard the king say to you and the others, 'Do not let anyone touch the young man Absalom.' If I had killed him I would surely have lost my own life. The king would have heard of it, and you yourself would have been the first to blame me."

Joab would not stop to listen. He hurried to the place where Absalom was hanging from the branches of a big oak tree. Joab took three darts and thrust them into the heart of the prince. Ten young men, Joab's bodyguard, closed in and killed Absalom. They took his body down from the tree and threw it into a pit.

Joab blew the trumpet to stop the battle. Now that Absalom was dead, there was no longer any cause for war.

As the clear notes of the trumpet resounded through the wood, the soldiers stopped fighting and gathered around Joab. Each man picked up a stone and threw it at the grave till Absalom was buried under an enormous heap of stones.

Ahimaaz, the young man who had brought tidings to King David about Absalom's doings, begged Joab to let him run to tell the king that the battle was won. Joab refused, for he knew that David would feel very sad when he heard that his son was dead. Another man was sent.

But Ahimaaz was young and eager to be the first to break the news to the king that the battle was won. Finally Joab gave in. Ahimaaz ran after the first messenger and soon overtook him.

King David was sitting in the gate of the city, waiting to hear news of the battle. A watchman stood on the roof over the gate. He called down to the king, "I see a man, all alone, running."

The king said, "If he is alone he has some news for us."

The watchman again called down to David, "I see another man running alone."

The king replied, "He also brings tidings."

The watchman called again, "I think the first one runs like Ahimaaz."

"He is a good man. He will bring good news," the king answered.

As soon as Ahimaaz came near enough to be heard, he shouted, "All is well!" He bowed and said, "Blessed be the Lord thy God, who has delivered up the men who were fighting against the king."

David asked, "Is the young man Absalom safe?"

"When Joab sent me, I saw a great tumult, but I did not know what it meant," Ahimaaz answered.

The king commanded, "Wait till this other messenger comes."

The other man came up, panting, "Tidings, my lord the king! The Lord has avenged you of all those who rose up against you!"

The king asked, "Is the young man Absalom safe?"

"May all the enemies of my lord the king be as that young man is," said the messenger.

Then the king was grief-stricken. He went upstairs to the little room over the gate, put his head down on his arms, and cried, "O my son Absalom, my son, my son Absalom! Would I had died for you, my son, my son!"

King David did not think of the victory and his kingdom. He thought only of his dear son.

The soldiers were coming back from the battle with joy in their hearts because their beloved king was safe. When they heard that pitiful cry, "O Absalom, my son, my son!" their joy was turned into sadness.

Joab, that stern and strong soldier, was David's true friend in his rough way. He said to David, "You have hurt all your soldiers, who have saved your life and the lives of your sons and your daughters and your wives. I see that you love your enemies and hate your friends. If Absalom had lived and all the rest of us had died, you would have been pleased.

"Get up and go out to the soldiers to thank them. Speak pleasantly to them, or all your people will leave you, and you will not have any friends left. That will be worse than any trouble you have ever had in your whole life."

This advice was not gentle, but it was very wise. King David wiped his eyes, went downstairs, and sat in the gate to greet his soldiers.

PART 3 — DAVID'S TRIUMPHANT RETURN

In a few days, throughout the land of Israel, the people began to say, "Our king, who saved us from the Philistines and from all our enemies, has fled out of the land on account of Absalom. But Absalom is dead now. Let us bring back our king to Jerusalem."

So David and all his household started to return to the royal city. The people of Judah were so delighted to have their beloved king back, that the whole tribe came to meet him at the River Jordan.

Ferry-boats carried the king and his followers over the river. What shouts of joy rang through the air, as David landed! What clapping of hands! The people ran along beside the king's procession, singing and dancing as they went.

There was one man who came to meet King David with fear and trembling instead of joy. This man was Shimei, who had thrown stones at David and cursed him when the king left the city. No wonder he came to meet David with fearful heart.

Shimei was one of the very first to speak to the king. He threw himself upon the ground and humbly begged the king to forgive him for behaving in so shameful a way.

"I know that I have sinned, and I am sorry for it now. I am the very first to meet the king. I beg the king to forget how I treated him."

David's general said, "Shimei ought to be put to death."

But David was so happy to see how all the people loved him that he did not want this happy day spoiled. He said to Shimei, "You shall not die."

Then Jonathan's lame son came to meet the king. David asked him, "Why didn't you go with me, Mephibosheth?"

"My servant has told lies about me. I did start to go, but I had to get an ass to ride upon, because I am lame," answered Mephibosheth.

As you remember, the king had told Ziba that he could have all his master's land. When King David heard from Mephibosheth himself that he had been his friend all the time, he said, "You and Ziba may divide the land."

Then Mephibosheth showed that he possessed some of his father Jonathan's sweet, unselfish nature, for he said, "Ziba may have all the land, for I am so happy that the king has come back again."

There was one man who had come with David to the river. This was Barzillai, the very old man who had sent David the fine present of food for his men. The king said to the old man, "Come back with me to Jerusalem, and live with me."

But Barzillai said, "I am an old man. How long have I to live? I am eighty years old. I should not enjoy life at the court. No, let me go back again to die in my own town. Here is my son; let him go with my lord."

So David kissed the good old man and blessed him. Barzillai went back to his own home, but his son went with David.

The people of Judah went with the king all the way to Jerusalem, shouting, singing, and clapping their hands, delighted to get their beloved king back again.

David sat upon his throne in Jerusalem. He praised God for helping him, singing,

> "He sent from on high, He took me;
> He drew me out of many waters.
> He delivered me from my strong enemy,
> And from them that hated me."

CHAPTER 76

The Wisest Man in the World

I Kings 1, 2, 3

Part 1 — The Anointing of Solomon

In his old age, when all was peaceful and his kingdom was easily governed by his helpers, King David spent his time getting everything ready for his son Solomon to build a beautiful temple to the Lord. God had not let David do this work because he was a man of war, but Solomon would be a man of peace. David collected great quantities of gold, silver, brass, iron, and precious stones to be used in the house of God.

There came a time when King David grew too old to attend to the affairs of the kingdom. One of his sons, Adonijah, thought that in this state of affairs he could easily become king.

Adonijah was the full brother of Absalom. He was very much like his brother, for he too was very handsome. He had fifty men to run before his chariot, so that the people would think him a great man.

Adonijah did not try to kill David, as Absalom had. He knew that his father could not live much longer. He thought, "Perhaps my father will not hear that I am trying to become king."

Some distance away from Jerusalem, Adonijah made a big feast, to which he invited all his brothers except Solomon. He did not want Solomon to know what he was doing, for he knew that David intended Solomon to be king after his own death. Adonijah probably intended to kill Solomon. He invited Joab, David's general, and Abiathar the priest to be present at this feast.

King David did not know what Adonijah was doing. Nathan the prophet heard about it, however. He went not to King David, but to

Solomon's mother, Bathsheba. He told her to go to the king and say to him, "My lord the king, didn't you promise me that my son Solomon should be king when you are dead? Then why is Adonijah reigning?"

Bathsheba went into the bedroom where King David was lying on a couch. As she bowed very low, the king asked her, "What do you wish?"

His wife said, "My lord, you promised that Solomon should reign after you, and now Adonijah has made himself king without letting you know. He has made a big feast, and has invited all your sons, and your captain Joab, and the priest Abiathar. Now, O king, all the people of Israel are waiting for you to tell them who shall be king after you. If you do not do something, then when you are dead, Solomon and I shall be killed."

While she was still talking to the king, Nathan the prophet came in. He bowed with his face to the ground, and repeated the news which Bathsheba had just told David.

King David saw that Solomon must be made king at once before he himself died, or there would be trouble for Solomon. He repeated his promise to Bathsheba that her son should be king.

Then he told his most trusted servants to anoint Solomon.

Nathan the prophet and Zadok the priest took Solomon out of the city. Zadok anointed Solomon with oil. They blew a trumpet. All the people came running to see what was going on.

When they heard the shout, "Long live King Solomon," then they all shouted too, "Long live King Solomon!" They joined the procession. Some of the soldiers marched ahead with trumpets. Then came Solomon riding on the king's mule, with soldiers marching on each side of him. Next came more soldiers, and all the people shouting, "Long live King Solomon!" The people were singing, dancing, piping on their flutes, and shouting so loudly that the earth echoed with the noise.

Adonijah and all his guests at the feast heard the great noise as the procession passed into Jerusalem. Joab, David's general, also heard the sound of the trumpet. He asked in alarm, "Why is this noise of the city in an uproar?"

The son of Abiathar the priest, who had so often brought messages to David during Absalom's rebellion, came to bring news to Adonijah. "Truly," he said, "our lord, King David, has made Solomon king. He has sent his body-guard of soldiers with him, and they have made him ride upon the king's mule. Zadok the priest and Nathan the prophet have anointed him. A great company of people are with him. They are shouting and singing and rejoicing, so that the city rings with the noise. This is what you have heard. King David's friends have accepted Solomon as their king."

When Adonijah's guests heard all this, they were afraid to stay. Every one of them quickly went home.

Adonijah was the most afraid of all, for he thought that if King Solomon caught him, he would surely kill him. Adonijah ran to the Tabernacle and caught hold of the horns of the altar, for he thought they would never dare to kill him there.

Some one brought word that Adonijah would not move away from the altar, unless King Solomon would promise not to kill him. Solomon sent word that if Adonijah would be a good man, he should not be killed; but if he behaved in a wicked way, he should die.

So Adonijah too acknowledged Solomon as king, bowing down before him.

PART 2 — How Solomon Got Wisdom

Before David died, he called a great meeting of all the chief men of Israel. When they had come together, he stood up and made a speech to them, telling them that God had chosen Solomon to be king and to build His house. He urged them to remember to keep all the commandments of the Lord.

Then David turned to Solomon, and in the presence of all that great company he said to him, "And you, Solomon my son, know the God of your father, and serve Him with a perfect heart and with a willing mind. For the Lord can read all your thoughts; if you come to

Him, He will be your God; if you forsake Him, He will cast you off forever."

Then David handed Solomon a plan to show him how to make the temple which God would help him build. He turned once more to the people, saying, "God has chosen my son to be king, but he is still young. It is a great work to build a house for the Lord God. As well as I was able, I have prepared for the building. I have gathered gold, silver, brass, iron, wood, marble, and precious stones. And now, who of you is willing to help? Who is willing to give a gift to God?"

All the people offered to help Solomon. They gave a great deal of gold and silver and iron. According to our present-day money, David and the men of Israel gave $1,710,000,000 in silver, and $2,737,500,-000 in gold.

There was great joy among the people. King David was glad to see the people offer so willingly to the Lord. He praised the Lord before all the people, thanking Him for all His kindness, and praying that Solomon and the people might remember to serve God.

And all the people blessed the Lord God of their fathers, and bowed their heads, and worshipped the Lord. The priests offered sacrifices. The people had a big feast and were very happy.

Solomon was placed before the people, and crowned king for the second time. He now was the ruler of the people. And he determined to keep the commandments of the Lord. God loved the young king who served Him so well.

Solomon made a great sacrifice, offering a thousand burnt offerings to God. That night God appeared to Solomon in a dream saying, "Ask what you would like to have Me give you."

Solomon said, "O Lord my God, Thou hast made me king instead of my father David. I feel as if I am only a little child. I do not know how to go out or how to come in. I have to rule over a people so great that they cannot be counted. Therefore give me, Thy servant, wisdom and knowledge, so that I may know how to rule Thy great people."

The Lord was pleased that Solomon had asked for wisdom, instead of riches, or honor, or victory over his enemies, or long life. God promised to give him wisdom and knowledge, so that he should be wiser than any other man before or after him.

God would also give him what he did not ask for, riches and honor. If Solomon would keep God's commandments, as David had, God would also give him long life.

Solomon awoke. It was a dream. But the dream was sent by God and came true; for Solomon became the wisest man who has ever lived in all the world. He was also very rich and highly honored, and he lived a long life.

Solomon spoke three thousand wise sayings, and he made a thousand songs. He knew all about trees, from the magnificent cedars of Lebanon to the tiny hyssop plant which springs out of a crack in the wall. He knew a great deal about animals, birds, creeping things, and fishes. People came from all over the world to listen to the wisdom of Solomon. Great kings visited him to hear him judge the people.

One day two women came to King Solomon with a dispute to be settled. One carried a living baby, and the other a dead child.

One of them said to the king, "O my lord, I live in the same house with this woman. I had a baby born to me; and after three days this other woman had a baby too. During the night, her child died, because she lay on it in her sleep. In the middle of the night she came and took my son out of my bed while I was sleeping, and put her dead child into my bed with me.

"In the morning when I awoke, I took up my baby. It was dead! When I looked closely at it, I saw that it wasn't mine at all, but hers. I saw that she had my baby in bed with her."

The second woman denied this. She cried loudly, "O king, she is not telling the truth! The living baby is mine, and the dead baby is hers!"

The first woman broke in again. "That isn't true. The dead baby is hers, and the living one is mine."

Who could tell which one was right? Both of them wanted the living child and refused the dead one.

The king said to one of his soldiers, "Bring me a sword." Then he commanded, "Divide the living child in two, and give half to one woman, and half to the other."

A soldier picked up the living baby, and raised up his sword to strike the child.

The true mother of the child raised a shriek. "O my lord, give her the living child! Do not kill it."

But the second woman said, "What you have decided is only fair. Divide it, and give us each half."

King Solomon said, "Give the living child to the first woman. She is its mother." So the baby was given to the woman who loved it.

When the people of Israel heard how wisely the king had judged, they realized that the wisdom of God was in him.

In the days of Solomon, the children of Israel increased in numbers until they were as many as the sand of the sea-shore. There was no war in his reign. All the people of Israel and Judah dwelt safely, every man in his own home, all the days of Solomon.

Solomon reigned over all the kingdoms that David had conquered, from the great River Euphrates in the north to the border of Egypt in the south. All the kings of these countries brought presents to him and served him.

CHAPTER 77

The Golden Kingdom of Solomon

I KINGS 6, 8, 9, 10; II CHRONICLES 2-7, 9

PART 1 — THE SPLENDID HOUSE OF GOD

In the fourth year of his reign Solomon began to build a temple for the Lord.

On the northern sea-coast, near the Lebanon mountains, was the great and important city of Tyre. Hiram, the king of Tyre, had always been a friend to King David.

Solomon sent a letter to him, saying, "You know that David my father could not build a house for the Lord, because of his many wars. But now the Lord has given me peace with all my neighbors. I am going to build a temple for God. It must be a great one, for our God is a great God.

"I beg you to send me cedar trees out of the mountains of Lebanon, where the wonderful cedars grow. You have men in your kingdom who understand how to chop down these trees. I will pay you for them by sending you wheat, and barley, and wine, and oil."

King Hiram answered thus:

"Because the Lord loved His people, He made you king over them. Blessed be the Lord God of Israel who has given to David a wise son. We will cut as much wood as you need, and send it to you in rafts to whatever place you choose."

Solomon numbered all the people of Canaan who were left of the heathen nations. He found them to be more than one hundred fifty thousand men. He sent them up into the country of King Hiram to be workmen for the building of the house of the Lord.

The building was covered with pure gold, both inside and out. The walls and the doors were ornamented with cherubim and palm trees and open flowers.

Inside, there was a Holy place and a Holy of Holies, as in the Tabernacle, but larger. The walls were carved with cherubim and flowers; and all were covered with gold. There were two cherubim for the Holy of Holies, much larger than the small ones that were over the Ark. These large cherubim were fifteen feet high. Their wings were spread out so that one cherub touched one wall and the other cherub touched the other wall, while their wings met in the middle of the room. The cherubim were overlaid with pure gold.

A beautiful curtain of fine blue, purple, and crimson linen was hung in front of the Holy of Holies. It was embroidered with cherubim.

There was one laver of brass for the priests to wash in. It was round, measuring fifteen feet across the top. It was held up by twelve figures of oxen, made of brass.

There were ten smaller lavers for washing the animals that were to serve for burnt offerings. Ten golden candlesticks furnished light for the temple. A hundred golden basins were made, as well as spoons, snuffers, censers, and other things.

Solomon made two great pillars of brass to stand in front of the Temple. The pillars were thirty-five feet high. They were beautifully decorated with wreaths of chains, brass lilies, and brass pomegranates.

The people worked for seven years to build the Temple. It was the most beautiful building in the land.

When all was finished, Solomon gathered all the important men of Israel in Jerusalem. They went to the tent where the Ark had been placed in David's time. They brought the holy Ark and all the holy dishes into the beautiful Temple.

All the priests and Levites were dressed in pure white linen. After they had placed the Ark in the Holy of Holies, they arranged themselves in a big choir. A band of cymbals, psalteries, and harps played as the choir sang to the Lord,

> "For He is good,
> And His mercy endureth forever."

The Temple was filled with a cloud, for the glory of the Lord shone brightly all around.

Solomon stood upon a platform where all the people could see him. After the singing, he kneeled down and spread forth his arms toward Heaven, praying aloud so that all the people could hear him.

Solomon knew that no building made by man can contain God, but he asked that God might hear him. He prayed that if the people should sin and repent, asking God's forgiveness, He would pardon them. Solomon also asked that if a stranger should pray toward the Temple, God would answer his prayer, so that all the people of the earth might honor the Lord.

When Solomon had finished his long prayer, he stood up. He blessed all the people of Israel, saying, "Blessed be the Lord, which hath given rest unto His people Israel. There hath not failed one word of all His good promise. The God of our fathers be with us, as He was with our fathers. Let Him not depart from us."

Solomon and all the people offered sacrifices to the Lord. After this worship, all the people of the land held a great feast, from the north to the south. Wherever Solomon ruled, this feast was held for two weeks.

The Lord appeared to Solomon in the night, saying to him, "I have heard your prayer, and I will do what you say. If I should punish My people because they have sinned against Me, and they become sorry for their sin and pray to Me, turning from their wicked ways, then I will forgive their sin. I have chosen and sanctified this house. It shall be Mine forever.

"And as for you, if you will walk before Me, as your father did, and if you will do all that I command you, then I will do to you as I promised your father. One of your children shall always be king.

"But if you forsake My laws to worship other gods, then I will take away the people out of this land which I have given them, and I will cast this house out of My sight; so that every one shall ask, 'Why has the Lord done this to this land and to this family?' And the answer shall be, 'Because they forsook the Lord God, and went and served other gods. That is the reason for this punishment.'"

PART 2 — THE VISIT OF A QUEEN

Besides being very wise, Solomon was also very rich. He lived in great magnificence.

After the beautiful Temple had been built, Solomon made a splendid palace for himself and another one for his wife, the daughter of the ruler of Egypt.

It took Solomon about twenty years to build the Temple, his own palace, and the palace for his wife. Then he built some wonderful cities in the mountains of Lebanon to the north, and in the heart of the desert. These cities were so well built that even today they are not wholly destroyed. When you are grown up, perhaps you will be able to go to that country and see their ruins.

Solomon gathered a large army of chariots and horses to defend his kingdom. He made a navy in a city on the Red Sea. These ships sailed around the country of Arabia to the land of Ophir, a land where gold was plentiful.

The ships brought back more than seven hundred thousand dollars' worth of gold to King Solomon. They also carried precious stones and almug wood, a rare wood out of which King Solomon made harps and psalteries for the temple singers. Once in three years Solomon's ships went to India, bringing back gold, silver, ivory, apes, and peacocks.

Jerusalem became a very splendid and rich city. Besides the Temple and the king's magnificent palace, there were many streets with beautiful houses. In the pleasant gardens peacocks strutted, spreading their gorgeous tails, while chattering monkeys swung from the palm-trees.

Inside the palace, King Solomon made a magnificent throne of ivory, covered with pure gold. There were six wide steps leading up to the throne. On each step there were two carved lions, one on each side, so that there was a row of lions on each side of the steps, twelve lions in all. There was no such throne in any other kingdom.

Solomon's magnificent court needed a good deal of food in one day: seven bushels of fine flour, fifteen bushels of meal, thirty oxen, one hundred sheep, and all kinds of deer and fowl.

King Solomon was wiser and richer than all the kings of the earth. From far countries men came to see King Solomon and to hear the wisdom that God had put into his heart. All these kings brought presents to king Solomon—gold and silver dishes, beautiful clothes, armor, delicious spices, horses, and mules.

More than a million dollars in gold came to King Solomon every year. All his cups and dishes were of pure gold; none were of silver. He made silver to be as common as stones in Jerusalem.

Solomon reigned over all the land from the Euphrates River to the border of Egypt, a kingdom three times as large as Saul's kingdom had been. And Solomon had peace on all sides.

Among the guests who came to hear the wisdom of King Solomon was a lady, the Queen of Sheba. Sheba was a rich country in far-away Arabia, on the shore of the Red Sea.

The Queen of Sheba travelled with great magnificence. She had a very great train of camels, for she had to journey about three hundred miles through the hot, sandy desert.

She wanted to talk to King Solomon, especially about his God. In her far-away country she had heard of Solomon's wisdom and of the mighty God of the Israelites.

When she came to Solomon, she asked him a great many questions. Solomon told her all she wanted to know. The Queen of Sheba tested his wisdom. She saw the houses that he had built, the delicious food of his table, the great number of his servants, and the magnificence of the Temple. She was astonished by all that she saw.

She said to King Solomon, "It was a true report that I heard in my own country of your wisdom and your doings. I did not believe it, until I came and saw with my own eyes. The half of it was not told me. Your wisdom and riches are far greater than I heard!

"Happy are your servants, who hear your wisdom all the time! Blessed be the Lord your God, who delighted to set you on the throne of Israel. It is because the Lord loved Israel that He has made you king."

The Queen of Sheba gave Solomon two hundred thousand dollars' worth of gold, and precious stones, and great abundance of the delicious spices which grew in her country. King Solomon gave the queen a present of every beautiful thing which she admired in his palace. Loaded down with presents, the queen and her servants went back to their own country.

CHAPTER 78

The Beginning of Bad Times

1 Kings 11, 12; II Chronicles 13

Part 1 — The Split in the Kingdom

In spite of all Solomon's wisdom, he did one very foolish and bad thing. That mistake brought about his downfall.

Solomon married many heathen women. He had seven hundred wives, many of whom were the daughters of heathen kings. His first wife had been the daughter of the ruler of Egypt. He had also married women of all the heathen Canaanites.

You will remember that God had strictly commanded the children of Israel that they should not marry heathen wives. Solomon was disobeying God when he did this.

In Solomon's old age his heathen wives turned away his heart from the true God, to heathen idols. Solomon built a place for the Moabite wives to worship their abominable god Chemosh, and right near Jerusalem he let his Ammonite wives worship their cruel idol Moloch. He built other places for all his heathen wives.

God was very angry with Solomon for doing this. The king had shamefully deserted his God, after the Lord had twice spoken directly to him.

Because the king did not keep the Lord's commandments, God would take the kingdom away from him. For the sake of David, He would not do this in Solomon's lifetime, but in the time of his son. He would leave one tribe for Solomon's son to rule, because He had promised that David's sons should rule forever.

One of Solomon's servants was a very able man named Jeroboam. One day God sent the prophet Ahijah to Jeroboam as he was walking in a field. The prophet came near to Jeroboam. Then he took hold of a new garment which he himself was wearing and tore it into twelve pieces.

Jeroboam was very much surprised to see the prophet do this strange thing. He was even more surprised when Ahijah said to him, "Take ten of these pieces, for God is going to take the kingdom away from King Solomon. He will give ten tribes of the children of Israel to you, and you shall be king over them. However, the Lord says, 'I will leave one tribe with David's family, because I have promised My servant David that his sons shall be kings forever in Jerusalem.'"

Solomon soon came to know that God was going to take the kingdom away from his son to give it to Jeroboam. Jeroboam had to flee to Egypt to save his life. He stayed there till Solomon was dead.

Solomon reigned forty years over Jerusalem. When at last he died and was buried with his fathers, his son Rehoboam reigned in his place.

As soon as Jeroboam heard that King Solomon was dead, he came back from Egypt. The people of Israel sent him with some of their chief men to ask a favor of the new king, Rehoboam.

The old prophet Samuel had warned them when they first asked for a king, that they would be sorry some day, for their king would make them work hard for him and pay high taxes. That warning had come true in the time of Solomon.

Now the people asked Rehoboam to make things a little easier for them. The new king did not know what answer to give them. He said, "Come again in three days, and I will give you an answer."

After the people's messengers were gone, King Rehoboam asked the old men who had been counselors to his father Solomon, what answer he should give. The wise counselors advised the king to answer the people nicely, for if he should promise to make things a little easier for them, then the people would love the king and be his servants forever.

Then the king asked the young men who were his companions and friends what answer they would advise him to give. These foolish young men, who had never had any experience in ruling a country, gave the opposite advice. They told him to answer that he would be even harder on the people than his father had been.

After three days the people came back, with Jeroboam at their head. The king answered them roughly, "My father made your burdens heavy, but I will make them heavier."

How foolish the young King Rehoboam was, to give the people such an answer as this! He certainly did not have his father's wisdom. When the people heard these proud words, they said, "What do we care for David or David's family? We won't have such a king!" They all left King Rehoboam and went home. There they crowned Jeroboam king.

Two of the tribes, Judah and Benjamin, stayed with Rehoboam. Judah was a very large tribe, but Benjamin was so small that it was counted with Judah as one.

There were now two kingdoms: Israel and Judah. They were never joined together again. The family of David ruled over Judah, but many different families of kings ruled over Israel.

PART 2 — HOW JEROBOAM MADE ISRAEL SIN

Jeroboam, the first king of Israel, was not a good king. The very first thing that he did was wrong.

He was afraid that many of the Israelites would become dissatisfied with him and would go back to Rehoboam, who was their rightful king, since he was a descendant of David. Jeroboam was especially afraid to have them go to Jerusalem to worship, for Rehoboam lived there.

To prevent the people's going to Jerusalem, Jeroboam made two golden calves. One of these calves he set up in Bethel, in the southern part of the kingdom; and the other in Dan, in the north. He proclaimed, "It is too long a journey to go all the way to Jerusalem to worship. I have made some gods nearer by. See these gods! These are the gods, O Israel, that brought you up out of the land of Egypt!"

Jeroboam made new priests. Anybody who wanted to could become a priest. He had only to bring a bullock and seven rams for a sacrifice, and then he became a priest.

Jeroboam created some feast-days too, so as to have the worship of the golden calves as much like the worship of the Lord as possible.

When the God-fearing people saw that Jeroboam was trying to lead them to worship idols, they left the country of Israel and moved down to Judah where the true God was worshiped. Of course, it was not easy for all of them to do this. They first had to sell their farms to get the money for travel. Perhaps some of them could not afford to leave their homes, and had to stay in the wicked kingdom of Israel, whether they wanted to or not.

On the other hand, there were also some of the people of Judah and Benjamin who were idol worshippers in secret. These people would rather live in Israel than in Judah.

Israel was weakened by having these people move in, and the good people move out. The priests and Levites had gone to Judah to live, too. They could not stay in Israel, where the king and the people were worshipping golden calves. So while Israel was weakened, Judah was strengthened.

I am very sorry to say that although King Rehoboam of Judah was good King David's grandson, yet he was not a very good man. His mother had been an Ammonite princess, one of King Solomon's heathen wives. She probably worshipped idols, and taught her son to worship them too.

King Rehoboam reigned for seventeen years. When he died, his son Abijah came to the throne of Judah.

Now Abijah was not pleased that Jeroboam had taken away all Israel, which he thought ought to be his kingdom. He was the great-grandson of David on both sides, for his mother was Absalom's daughter and his father Rehoboam was Solomon's son. Abijah considered himself the rightful ruler over all the tribes.

In order to get all the kingdom together again, Abijah went to war with Jeroboam. He could gather only four hundred thousand soldiers to go against Jeroboam's army of eight hundred thousand men.

Before the battle, King Abijah went to a high place, where Jeroboam and all his soldiers could see and hear him. He shouted across to them, saying that God had given the kingdom of Israel to David and to his sons forever, and that Jeroboam had no right to be king.

He reminded them that they had turned away from their rightful king and from the true God to worship golden calves. They had sent the priests of God away from their country, making a priest of anyone who wanted to become a priest. How could they succeed when they had done all these wicked things? In Judah, the sons of Aaron, the true priests, burned sweet incense to God every morning and evening, and offered sacrifices in the way that God commanded. God Himself was with the men of Judah; and His priests were there to sound the trumpets against Jeroboam.

Jeroboam, instead of listening to this warning, took some of his soldiers and crept around behind the armies of Judah, while King Abijah was talking. He did not care anything about the true God. He had twice as many soldiers as King Abijah had; so he was sure he would win. He had more faith in a large number of soldiers, than in asking God for help.

After King Abijah had finished talking, he turned around. What should he see but the Israelite soldiers both before and behind him!

The soldiers of Judah trusted in God. They cried to Him for help. While the soldiers shouted, the priests sounded the trumpets. As they shouted, God smote Jeroboam and all Israel. The soldiers of Israel ran away from the soldiers of Judah. God gave the men of Judah a great victory. Five hundred thousand of the soldiers of Israel were killed.

Abijah pursued Jeroboam, capturing a number of cities — Bethel and all the southern part of Ephraim. So Abijah proved that it is better to trust in the Lord than in great multitudes of soldiers.

Abijah died when he had reigned only three years. His son Asa was made king after him, while Jeroboam was still ruling in Israel.

CHAPTER 79

The Divided Kingdom

I KINGS 13-16; II CHRONICLES 14, 15

Kings of Israel	*Kings of Judah*
Jeroboam	Rehoboam
Nadab	Abijah
Baasha	Asa
Elah	
Zimri	
Omri	
Ahab	

PART 1 — THE BAD KINGS OF ISRAEL

Jeroboam, who led Israel to worship idols, reigned for a long time. One day as he stood by the heathen altar which he had made for the worship of the golden calf, there came a prophet sent by the Lord from the country of Judah.

The prophet declared that one day there would be born a king of David's family, whose name would be Josiah. This king would kill the priests of this altar which Jeroboam had built, and would destroy the altar.

Three hundred years later this prophecy came true. A king of David's line, named Josiah, did indeed go through all the land to destroy the heathen altars.

Perhaps this prophecy frightened Jeroboam. A short time later, his son became very ill, and seemed about to die. But Jeroboam did not go to the golden calves. He did not pray to them to make his child better. Although he had made these calves for the Israelites to worship, he himself did not believe in them.

Jeroboam told his wife to dress like an ordinary lady, so that no one would know that she was the king's wife, and to go to the prophet Ahijah to ask him whether the child would live or die.

This was the prophet who had foretold that Jeroboam was to be king over Israel, by tearing his new garment into twelve pieces and giving Jeroboam ten pieces. Ahijah was now very old and almost blind, but God told him who was coming, and what he must say to her.

As soon as Jeroboam's wife came to the door, the old prophet called out, "Come in, you wife of Jeroboam! I have bad news for you. God raised Jeroboam up to be king over His people Israel, taking away the kingdom from David's family.

"But Jeroboam has done more wickedness than any other king, in making heathen gods and in turning away from the Lord. Tell Jeroboam that for all this, God will punish him. The child who is sick shall die and be buried. He is the only one of your whole family who shall ever be buried. Those of Jeroboam's family that die in the city shall be eaten by the dogs, and those that die in the field shall be eaten by the birds of the heavens.

"God will soon raise up a king over Israel who will destroy the house of Jeroboam. He will punish His people Israel for worshipping idols. He will root up Israel out of this good land and will scatter them beyond the River Euphrates.

"Now arise and go home, you wife of Jeroboam. When your feet enter the city, your child shall die."

Jeroboam's wife went home to carry the terrible news to her guilty husband. As she entered the city, the child died. He was buried, and all Israel mourned for him.

Soon after the death of his son, sinful Jeroboam died. His son Nadab, who was just as bad as his father, came to be king.

Nadab was king for only two years. Then a man named Baasha killed Nadab and made himself king over Israel. Baasha killed every man of the family of Jeroboam, as God had told the prophet. This was God's punishment to wicked Jeroboam for all his sins.

Baasha was not a good king. He had begun his reign by murdering the whole family of Jeroboam. He went on worshipping idols and the golden calves. He made Israel worship the golden calves and the idols, just as Jeroboam had done.

It was no wonder that the good people in Israel did not wish to stay where such wicked things were going on.

Baasha tried to stop the God-fearing people in Israel from going down to Judah to live. He fortified one of the cities on the border between Israel and Judah. Baasha meant to put soldiers there to prevent the people from leaving his country. But he did not succeed.

God was angered by the wickedness and idolatry of this king. He sent a prophet to him to say that because Baasha had made Israel sin, as Jeroboam had done, God would punish him as He had punished Jeroboam. Those of Baasha's family who should die in the city would be eaten by the dogs, and those that should die in the country, the vultures would eat.

Soon after this prophecy, Baasha died, and his son Elah came to be king of Israel.

PART 2 — A HAPPY LAND AND AN UNHAPPY ONE

All this time, good King Asa was reigning in Judah. He destroyed all the idols that he could find, and he commanded the people of Judah to worship the Lord.

For ten years, there was no war in Judah. King Asa built high stone walls around many of his cities, to make them strong if ever a war should come. He trained a big army of soldiers for defense.

After he had reigned in peace for ten years, a great army of a million black men came up out of Ethiopia, which was a country in Africa, south of Egypt, where black people lived.

Did King Asa put his trust in his trained soldiers? No, he did not. He asked the Lord to help him. God listened to Asa's prayer. He gave the king and his men a great victory.

The fleeing Ethiopians left behind many fine things in their tents which the men of Judah took for themselves. Cattle, sheep, and camels they also left behind. The people of Judah were richer after the war than they had been before. Again they had peace, for the enemies around them had learned to leave God's people alone.

The Lord sent a prophet to good King Asa, promising that the Lord would be with Asa as long as the king trusted in God. Asa had begun his reign by trying to do right and to please God. It encouraged him very much to hear the prophet say that God had seen it and was pleased, and to have the prophet tell him that God would reward his good work. So now he decided to go on, and do still more for the Lord.

He had all the people of Judah and Benjamin come together for an outdoor meeting under the blue sky. A great many of the people of the tribes of Ephraim, Manasseh, and Simeon came to him also. They saw that he was a king who was trying to do right, and to serve God, and that God was helping him.

At this big meeting, the people made a big sacrifice and worshipped God. They promised to serve the God of their fathers with all their hearts and with all their souls.

They decided that everybody who would not serve God should be put to death, for they were determined to root out all the idol worship in Judah. In unison they shouted their oath to serve God. The trumpets and cornets rang out at the same time. The people clapped their hands, just as happy as they could be. They were serving the true God, and nothing makes people so happy as to know that they are doing what God wants them to do.

God gave the people of Judah peace, and no nation came to make war against them. But meanwhile, very bad things were going on in Israel. It was no wonder that God-fearing people did not wish to live there.

King Jeroboam had died. His son Nadab had proved to be just as bad as his father Jeroboam, and after only two years he had been killed by Baasha. Baasha had killed not only the king, but every man who was left of wicked Jeroboam's family.

Baasha, who had no right to rule, was a wicked king also. He soon died, and his son Elah came to the throne. Neither did Elah live very long. He was sinful, like all the other kings of Israel. One day when he was drunk, his servant Zimri came in and murdered Elah, and made himself king. Zimri killed all Baasha's relations, just as Baasha had murdered all the family of Jeroboam.

Although Zimri committed all these murders in order to make himself king, it did him very little good, for he was king for only one week. The people did not want him to be king. They chose Omri, who was the captain of the soldiers. With his soldiers, Omri went to fight against the king's city, where Zimri was. When Zimri heard that the city was overcome, he went into his palace and set it on fire. He was burned to death in the ruins of his palace.

Omri now became king of Israel. He was more wicked than any of the other kings who had ruled over Israel. After he had reigned for twelve years, he died and his son Ahab became king.

Ahab was even worse than his father had been. He was the most wicked king that Israel ever had. His wife Jezebel was just as bad as he. She was the daughter of the heathen king of Sidon, who was a priest of the idol Baal.

Ahab built a temple for Baal in Samaria, the royal city, and he set up the heathen Asherah. Queen Jezebel had four hundred heathen priests for the Asherah, and Ahab had four hundred fifty priests for the worship of the idol Baal.

There were still a few priests of God in Israel who tried to keep the people from worshipping idols. Jezebel tried to kill these priests of the true God. She hated the Lord, and did all she could to root out the worship of Jehovah, so that Israel would become a heathen country.

Jezebel had as a servant in her household a very remarkable man named Obadiah. He was ruler over the royal house.

Obadiah was a good man. He tried to serve God and to keep the Israelites from worshipping idols. When Jezebel tried to kill the priests of the Lord, Obadiah hid one hundred priests in caves and fed them at his own expense.

With this wicked king and queen on the throne, the country of Israel had become almost heathen. In those days, when God was forgotten in the land, a certain man did a thing that God had forbidden the children of Israel five hundred years earlier.

Do you remember that when the walls of Jericho fell down, and the city was burned with fire, God commanded Joshua to curse the city? Joshua said to the Israelites, "Cursed be the man before the Lord that rises up and builds this city Jericho. When he lays the foundations his oldest son shall die; and when he sets up the gates, his youngest son shall die."

For five hundred years the children of Israel observed this word. But in the days of King Ahab one man was so rash as to rebuild the city of Jericho. When he laid the foundations, his oldest son died, and when he put up the gates, his youngest son died, just as Joshua had foretold.

CHAPTER 80

Elijah, the Stern Prophet

I Kings 17, 18, 19

King of Israel	*King of Judah*
Ahab	Asa

Part 1 — Why the King Became Angry

Was God going to allow all the Israelites to forget Him and to become idolaters?

No, indeed. God raised up a prophet named Elijah, one of the greatest prophets that ever lived. The Lord sent this man to King Ahab, to tell him that God was going to punish him for his idolatry.

Elijah lived on the east side of the Jordan River. When God gave him the message for Ahab, the stern and angry prophet crossed the river into Samaria. Up the marble steps of the magnificent palace he strode, into the very presence of the king. Lifting his hands to the sky, he said in a solemn and ringing voice, "As the Lord God of Israel lives, before whom I stand, there shall not be rain or dew these years, until I say it shall come."

Then Elijah turned away from the wicked king and marched out of the palace.

God spoke to Elijah, saying to him, "Go away from here. Hide yourself near the brook Cherith, close to the Jordan. You can drink the water of the brook and eat the food which I have commanded the ravens to bring to you."

So Elijah lived by the brook, hiding away from the angry king. For Ahab would have cut off Elijah's head if he had found him.

After a time the brook dried up, because there had been no rain. The Lord commanded Elijah to go north to the town of Zerephath which did not belong to Israel. God had commanded a widow there to take care of the prophet.

Elijah immediately left the dried-up brook, and started on the long journey to Zerephath, more than one hundred miles to the north. It must have been a hard journey. Elijah had to go all the distance on foot. He had to travel secretly, hidden away from the people, for the king was hunting all over the country to find the prophet. Ahab wanted to kill him, for he thought that Elijah was responsible for the lack of rain.

As he travelled across the land, Elijah could see the bare and brown fields where everything had shrivelled. Every day the sun rose blazing hot and travelled across the sky scorching everything; and every day the sky was like copper, with never a sign of a mist or a cloud.

At last, after travelling the long weary way, Elijah passed out of the country of the Israelites into the country of Sidon, and came to the town of Zerephath.

When he came to the gate of the city, he saw the widow gathering a few sticks to make a little fire.

He asked her to bring him a drink of water. When she started to get it, he called to her, "Please bring a little piece of bread too."

The woman replied, "As the Lord your God lives, I have not a single loaf of bread in the house. I have only a little meal in a barrel, and a little olive oil in a jug. I have come out to gather a few sticks to make a fire, so that I can make a last cake of the meal and olive oil, for my son and me. After that is eaten, we shall have nothing more, and we shall have to starve."

Elijah said to her, "Do not worry, for the God of Israel says that the barrel of flour and the jug of oil will last all the time, till I send rain upon the earth."

So the woman made Elijah a little cake first. Then she made one for herself and her son. It happened as the prophet said. No matter how often she baked bread, the flour in the barrel did not give out, and neither did the jug of oil. There was always plenty left. This was a miracle, something that only the mighty power of God can bring about. God gave his prophet Elijah power to work marvelous miracles.

Some time after this, the woman's young son became very sick. He finally died. The woman thought that her son's death was a punishment for some sin which she had done. She came to Elijah in sorrow. "O thou man of God, did you come here to punish me for my sin by killing my son?"

"Give the boy to me," Elijah commanded. Taking the little boy out of his mother's arms, he carried him upstairs into his own bedroom. He laid him upon the bed.

Elijah called to God, praying, "O Lord, my God, let this child's soul come into him again."

What a strange thing to ask! Never had anyone who was dead come to life again! Yet Elijah had faith that God could do it. He lay down on the boy's body, and stretched himself over the little child. Three times he did this.

God listened to Elijah's prayer. The child's soul came into him again. He started to breathe. Elijah carried him to his mother and said to her, "See, your boy is living again!"

The happy mother flung her arms around her dear little boy, kissed him, and hugged him. She exclaimed to Elijah, "I know now that you are truly a man sent from God."

PART 2 — WHO SHALL BE GOD?"

Three years passed without rain. Month after month slipped by, and not a drop of rain fell out of the sky. Day after day the sun rose and sent its scorching beams down on a parched earth. Day after day the people scanned the copper sky for the least sign of a cloud, but none appeared.

The rivers ran low and then dried up. The fields lay baked and brown under the blazing sun. The animals could not find a blade of grass. They were starving for something to eat.

The little food that the people had was almost gone. They were suffering from hunger.

King Ahab said to Obadiah, the ruler of his house, "Let us go out into the country, where the brooks and springs are, and see if we can find a little grass for the horses and mules, so that they do not all die." In order to cover the whole country, Ahab and Obadiah went in different directions.

At this time Elijah was still living with the widow in Zarephath. God said to him, "Go show yourself to Ahab. I will send rain on the earth."

Therefore Elijah went down into the land of Israel. Out in the country he came upon Obadiah, who was looking for grass. Obadiah was completely surprised to see Elijah, for King Ahab had hunted everywhere to find Elijah, whom he blamed for the famine. Every part of the country had been searched, but Elijah could not be found. And now here he was!

Bowing down to the ground, Obadiah asked, "Is it possible that you are my lord Elijah?"

Elijah answered, "I am Elijah. Go and tell the king that I am here."

Obadiah answered, "I dare not tell him, for he has hunted for you everywhere. He made the people swear by an oath that you were not in their homes. You say, 'Go tell King Ahab that Elijah is here.' But as soon as I go to tell him, the Spirit of the Lord will carry you away somewhere else. When I come and tell Ahab, and he cannot find you, he will kill me.

"I have been a worshipper of God since my youth. Did no one tell you what I did when Jezebel killed the prophets of the Lord? I took a hundred of them, hid them in two caves and fed them with bread and water. Do you repay me for this by sending me with a message which will make Ahab want to kill me?"

But Elijah promised, "As truly as the Lord God of Israel lives, today I will show myself to Ahab."

Then Obadiah went to meet King Ahab and told him that Elijah had been found. As soon as Ahab saw Elijah, he asked, "Are you the one who is troubling Israel?"

Elijah spoke sternly. "I have not troubled Israel. You and your wicked father have troubled Israel, because you have forsaken the commandments of the Lord and have worshipped Baal. Now gather all the people of Israel to Mount Carmel. Bring the four hundred fifty prophets of Baal and the four hundred prophets of the Asherah."

Ahab sent messengers throughout the land of Israel for the people to come to Mount Carmel to meet the prophet Elijah. The people gathered at the mountain. Ahab brought the prophets of Baal and of the Asherah.

Elijah stood up boldly before all the people. In a ringing voice he cried out to them, "How long are you going to be undecided? If the Lord is God, follow Him; but if Baal, then follow him."

All the people answered him never a word. They knew that they had left their God to follow Baal. Shame covered their faces. Perhaps some of them wished to say, "We will follow the Lord," but they dared not say anything in the presence of the king and the eight hundred fifty prophets.

There stood the brave prophet, alone on one side, with the great host of people and the eight hundred fifty prophets of Baal and the Asherah on the other side. Again the prophet's voice rang out over the mountain.

"I am the only prophet of the Lord, but Baal's prophets are four hundred fifty men. Let them give us two bullocks for sacrifice. Let Baal's prophets choose one bullock, lay it on wood, and put no fire under it. I shall prepare the other bullock and put it on wood, but set no fire under it. Then let the prophets of Baal call on the name of your gods, and I shall call on the name of the Lord. The god that answers by fire, let him be God."

The people raised a shout, "Yes, that is right! Let us do that!"

PART 3 — FIRE FROM HEAVEN

Which prayer would be answered?

The heathen priests took the bullock which was brought to them. While the host of people watched with the most intense excitement, the bullock was made ready.

Then the priests of Baal ran around and around the altar in a frenzy of excitement, jumping and leaping on the altar, cutting themselves with knives till blood gushed, shouting and screaming and howling, "O Baal, hear us! O Baal, hear us!"

But there was no answer by fire.

After the priests had shouted to Baal all morning without an answer, Elijah began to make fun of them. He shouted mockingly, "Cry louder! He is a god. Perhaps he is talking, or he is on a journey, or perhaps he is asleep and must be waked. Cry louder! Make him hear you!"

The frantic prophets screamed and howled, "O Baal, hear us!" They ran around in a frenzy, cutting themselves with their knives. They kept this up all day long. By evening there was no breath left in them. Still there was no answer from Baal.

When it was evening, the waiting people had become tired of watching the frantic priests leaping and cutting themselves. At last Elijah commanded the people, "Come near to me." They all came as near as they could.

Elijah found an old altar of the Lord that had been broken down. With twelve large stones he built up this altar in the name of the Lord.

He cut the bullock in pieces and laid it on the wood. He dug a little ditch around the altar and then, so that the people could see that he was perfectly honest and was playing no tricks, he said, "Fill four jars with water, and pour it on the sacrifice and on the wood of the altar."

Mount Carmel was close by the sea, so that water was quickly brought. Elijah said, "Do it a second time." And they did it a second time. Then he said, "Do it a third time." And they did it the third time. The water ran round about the altar, soaking everything and filling the ditch.

When everything was ready, Elijah lifted up his face to Heaven. He prayed very solemnly.

More than sixty years had passed since the kingdom of Israel had separated from the kingdom of Judah, and since the kingdom of Israel had been led into idol worship by their wicked kings. The old people could remember when Solomon was king, and when all the tribes of Israel went up to Jerusalem to worship God. Many of the younger people were hearing a public prayer to God for the very first time, although they had heard many prayers to the idol Baal. When they heard Elijah begin to pray so solemnly and earnestly, they were very much impressed.

Elijah prayed, "Lord God of Abraham, Isaac, and Israel, let it be known that Thou art God in Israel, and that I am Thy servant, and that I have done all these things at Thy word. Hear me, O Lord, hear me; that this people may know that Thou art the Lord God and that Thou hast turned their heart back again."

When Elijah prayed, suddenly the fire of God fell upon the altar. It burned the bullock and the wood. In a minute, the whole altar was ablaze. The fire was so hot that the water in the trenches boiled away. The stones of the altar and the ground around the altar burned.

The astonished people fell on their knees and cried out, "Jehovah, He is God! Jehovah, He is God!" When they saw the power of their own God, they became disgusted with the false heathen idol, and with the senseless screaming of the heathen prophets.

Then Elijah commanded them to capture all the prophets of Baal. He brought the prophets down to the brook Kishon and slew them there.

Then he said to Ahab, "Go, eat and drink, for there is a sound of abundance of rain."

Elijah himself went to the top of Mount Carmel and threw himself down upon the ground and prayed. He said to his servant, "Go up and look toward the sea."

The servant went and looked. He came back to Elijah, saying, "There is nothing."

Seven times Elijah told his servant to look toward the sea. When the servant came back the seventh time, he said, "A little cloud as big as a man's hand is rising up out of the sea."

Elijah commanded him, "Go tell Ahab, 'Get your chariot ready and hurry home before the rain stops you.'"

The heavens became black with clouds and wind. There was a great rain. Elijah tucked up his robe into his girdle and ran before Ahab's chariot all the way into Jezreel, through the midst of the heavy rain which had come in answer to his prayers.

PART 4 — GOD COMFORTS ELIJAH

Queen Jezebel was not present when Elijah called down fire from heaven. When Ahab told her that Elijah had killed the prophets of Baal and the Asherah, Jezebel was furiously angry. She sent a messenger to Elijah to tell him that she was going to kill him.

Elijah left the royal city in a great hurry. He went south to the country of Judah. He was still afraid to stop; he left his servant there, and went a day's journey farther into the wilderness.

Then he could go no farther. He was tired and discouraged. He had hoped that the people of Israel were going to turn back to God. Now he saw that as long as wicked Queen Jezebel was on the throne, there was very little chance that they would serve Jehovah.

Poor Elijah sat down under a juniper tree. He felt too tired to live. All that he had done was of no use, he thought. He asked the Lord to let him die. The tired prophet, who had been walking night and day without food or drink, was so exhausted that he fell asleep under the juniper tree.

But God was taking tender care of His tired servant, who had acted so bravely at Mount Carmel. While Elijah was sleeping, an angel touched him and said, "Arise and eat."

When Elijah awoke from his sleep, he saw a cake baked on the coals, and a bottle of water. He ate and drank, for he was hungry and thirsty after his long journey. He had been afraid to stop long enough to get much to eat.

After eating and drinking, he lay down once more and slept again. The angel again touched him and said, "Arise and eat, for the journey is too long for you."

Elijah had slept so long that he was thoroughly rested. He sat up and ate again, till his hunger was entirely satisfied.

Strengthened by that food, the prophet travelled for forty days and nights. Farther and farther south he went, through the terrible desert over which the children of Israel had travelled during the forty years of their wanderings. At last he came near the mountain of Sinai, where God had given the Ten Commandments to Moses and the children of Israel.

Here Elijah was safe from Jezebel. He found a cave in which to live. After a time, God spoke to him, asking "What are you doing here, Elijah?"

Elijah answered, "I have worked hard for the Lord God of hosts, but the children of Israel have forsaken Thee and have thrown down Thine altars, and have killed Thy prophets with the sword. I only am left. They are trying to kill me too."

"Go and stand upon the mountain before the Lord," came the command.

So Elijah went upon the mountain. A terrible wind came up. It was so strong that it broke great pieces off the mountain, and cracked great rocks open. But the Lord was not in the wind. After the wind had gone down, there came a dreadful earthquake. The whole mountain shook and trembled. But the Lord was not in the earthquake. After the earthquake, there came a fire. But the Lord was not in the fire.

Elijah stood there and saw the terrible hurricane shrieking around the mountain, uprooting trees and breaking the great rocks; then the dreadful earthquake, making the solid mountain shake and tremble; and then the furious fire, raging among the trees of the mountains. He understood the strength and power of his God, and he realized that his God was much stronger than wicked Ahab and Jezebel, or all the wicked people in the world.

After the wind and earthquake and fire, Elijah heard a still, small voice. Elijah knew immediately that it was God speaking to him, gently and kindly. God asked, "What are you doing here, Elijah?"

Elijah answered as he had the first time, telling how the Israelites were killing all God's prophets. What was the use of trying?

But the Lord commanded him to return to the country of Israel. He must go to the city of Damascus and anoint a new king over the country of Syria, instead of Ben-hadad who was ruling there. Then he had to anoint a new king over Israel instead of Ahab. Last of all, he had to anoint a new prophet to fill his own place and to do his work after his death.

Then God told Elijah that he was mistaken in thinking that he was the only one in the whole country of Israel who was true to God. There were still seven thousand who had not bowed to Baal.

Seven thousand others who were true to God! That encouraged Elijah. And to think that Ahab would not be king much longer — that made him glad. And then to know that his hard work as prophet was almost finished — that made him happy too.

It was hard to be a prophet of God in those wicked days, and to have to stand up for God all alone when everybody else was worshipping idols. Elijah was very brave and courageous. He had dared to come before a wicked and idolatrous king, and to proclaim the true God, and then to put all the prophets of Baal to death. Yet he was very glad to know that he would not have to live much longer in this wicked world.

(Oh, Elijah, Elijah, do not be afraid! What if Jezebel says she will kill you? She will never be able to do it. Though she sends men with swords all over the land, you will never die at her hand! The mighty God is taking care of you. The chariot of God is coming for you, Elijah! Jezebel can do nothing. God has appointed that you are not to die. Like Enoch of old, you are going to Heaven without passing through the gates of death that must close on all the rest of us. Your life has been hard, but soon the chariot of God is coming for you.)

As God directed, Elijah left the cave in Mount Sinai and started on his long journey. When at last he reached the land of Israel, he saw a man named Elisha ploughing a field with twelve yoke of oxen. Elijah did not stop to speak to him. As he passed by, he threw his mantle over Elisha's shoulders without saying a word.

Elisha knew what that meant. It meant he had been chosen to follow Elijah and to be prophet after him. He ran after Elijah and said, "Let me first go and tell my father and mother, and kiss them good-bye. Then I will come and follow you."

Elisha lived with Elijah from that time on. He waited on the old prophet and took care of him. It was pleasant for Elijah to have a friend and companion to talk to and pray with. And Elisha had a wonderful teacher to show him how to become a prophet of the true God.

CHAPTER 81

Stories About Israel's Wicked King

I KINGS 20, 21

King of Israel	*King of Judah*
Ahab	Jehoshaphat

PART 1 — GOD HELPS AHAB

North of the kingdom of Israel was the great kingdom of Syria. It was much larger than Israel. Its king was Ben-hadad.

King Ben-hadad gathered his soldiers together and made war against Israel. With him went thirty-two other kings, who had horses and chariots. This great host of soldiers and chariots and horses went up to Samaria, the capital city of Ahab. They surrounded the city and besieged it.

When Ahab saw the great host of soldiers surrounding Samaria, he was terrified. The king of Judah had strengthened his country and gathered an army of a million trained soldiers. But Ahab had done nothing to protect his country. He had only seven thousand soldiers.

King Ben-hadad was a proud and cruel king. He sent a very insulting message to King Ahab: "Thus says the great King Ben-hadad, 'Your silver and your gold belong to me. Your wives and your children, even the very best of them belong to me.'"

King Ahab shook with terror. What should he do? He had no God to go to. He and Queen Jezebel had torn down the altars of God; Jezebel had killed the prophets of God whenever she could find them. Baal had taken the place of the Lord God of Israel. Should they go to their idol for help? Ah, no, even Ahab knew better than to go to Baal.

He could do nothing but submit. His army was not strong enough to fight against Ben-hadad, who had thirty-two kings with horses and chariots, and thousands and thousands of soldiers. He sent a humble reply to King Ben-hadad, saying, "My lord, O king, as you have said, I belong to you, with all that I have."

Was Ben-hadad satisfied with this humble answer?

He was a bully. He knew that King Ahab with his few soldiers could do nothing against him. So he sent King Ahab another insulting message. "Tomorrow I am going to send my servants to hunt all over your house and the houses of your servants. They will take away every nice thing that you have."

This time King Ahab called all the elders of the land together and told them what Ben-hadad said. All the men said, "Do not listen to him."

King Ahab finally plucked up a little spirit and sent this word to Ben-hadad: "All that you asked of me in the first place I will do, but this last demand I will not submit to."

That was just what Ben-hadad wanted. Now he had a good excuse to pounce on Ahab. He and his thirty-two kings would go up and crush Ahab and his soldiers to powder. He answered boastfully that there would not be enough left of Samaria for each of Ben-hadad's soldiers to have a handful of dust.

Ahab, now that he had the elders of his kingdom behind him, was a little more courageous. Instead of sending a humble answer, he told Ben-hadad not to boast before the battle had been fought.

When Ben-hadad heard this scornful answer, he and the thirty-two kings were drinking. Nevertheless, he said to the kings, "Get yourselves ready to go to war against the city."

Ben-hadad and his thirty-two kings would probably have crushed Ahab and his seven thousand soldiers just as they planned, if something had not happened to prevent it. The mighty God came to help Ahab. He sent a prophet to the king, saying that He would help the Israelites.

Ahab asked, "Who shall do the fighting?"

The prophet said, "The young princes."

Ahab sent word quickly for all the young princes to come to him. How many do you think there were? Only two hundred thirty-two!

By noon the Israelites were ready. The little army of seven thousand soldiers ventured out of the city to go against the hosts of the Syrians.

Ben-hadad and his thirty-two kings were drinking in their tents. Someone brought the news that soldiers were coming out of the city of Samaria. Ben-hadad, half drunk as he was, did not trouble himself. He gave an order, "Whether they have come out for peace or for war, take them alive."

Why did Ben-hadad want the men to be taken alive?

In those days, people liked to torture their captives before killing them. Nowadays the love of Jesus Christ has made men kinder. We hate to see suffering. But at that time, people enjoyed making others suffer.

The Israelites were very brave because they knew that the God of their fathers was helping them. Every one of the two hundred thirty-two princes, and each of the seven thousand soldiers picked out a Syrian soldier and fought him.

When the Syrian soldiers saw the courage of the Israelite men, they soon gave way. The poor heathen soldiers had no God to help them; and even their king, who should have been leading his soldiers, was drunk. That large army became a mere rabble of terrified and fleeing soldiers. Even King Ben-hadad got on a horse and galloped away. The Israelites chased after the Syrians and killed many more of them.

Why had God helped the wicked King Ahab, who had forgotten the Lord and torn down His altars, and had worshipped the idol Baal?

There were two reasons: Although the Israelites had forgotten God, they were His people. God loved them, and He did not want them to be destroyed utterly. There were still seven thousand of the people who had not worshipped Baal. Perhaps some of the others would turn back to God when they saw how God helped them against their enemies.

The other reason was this: Although the Hebrews were God's special people, yet all the earth is God's. The Syrians, who lived right next to the Israelites, must have learned something about their wonderful God. The Lord wanted the Syrians, and all the nations of the earth to know Him.

PART 2 — HOW AHAB TREATED GOD'S ENEMY

With God's help, the Israelites had crushed the Syrians and sent them back. The Lord sent a prophet to King Ahab with this message: "Next year King Ben-hadad will come back. Make your army and your kingdom strong, so as to be ready for him."

When King Ben-hadad returned to Damascus with the remnant of his army, his servants said to him, "The god of the Israelites is a god of the hills. We made a mistake in fighting against them in the hill country. Let us go and fight them next year in the open, on the plains. Gather another army just as large as the one which we have lost. Give the command to captains who understand how to manage soldiers. If we fight on the plains we shall surely be able to overcome them."

Ben-hadad did all this. The next year he returned to make war against the Israelites. This time he did not go so far as Samaria, for that city was on a hill. He went only to the lowlands just east of the Sea of Galilee.

The children of Israel were able to gather only a small army to meet the great host of the Syrians. But again a prophet came to King Ahab and said, "Because the Syrians have said, 'The Lord is a god of the hills but not of the valleys,' God will deliver all this multitude into your hand, so that all people may know that He is Lord over all the earth."

And again the Israelites were victorious in a great battle. Though it is hard to believe, one hundred thousand Syrian soldiers died that day in the battle.

The rest of the Syrians fled to a city nearby, thinking to find safety there. Many more of them lost their lives, for the city wall fell upon them and killed twenty-seven thousand.

What became of King Ben-hadad?

The king fled into a house and hid himself in an inner room. He knew the Israelites would soon find him and kill him. Soon, however, some of his servants came to him and said, "We have heard that the kings of Israel are merciful kings. Let us wear sackcloth and put ropes on our heads, and go to the king of Israel. Perhaps he will save your life."

Ben-hadad knew that there was no other way. He let his servants put rough sack-cloth on their bare skins and ropes on their heads. They went to King Ahab and said, "Thy servant Ben-hadad says, 'I pray thee, let me live!'"

Ahab replied, "Is he still alive? He is my brother." He sent for Ben-hadad and invited him to come up into the chariot with him. He made friends with him, and let him go.

How very foolish and wrong of Ahab! Ben-hadad was a very evil king. God wanted him punished by death.

God sent a prophet to Ahab to say, "Because you have let this man go, you shall die in his stead."

Ahab went home to his house in Samaria, displeased. Although he had put God out of his thoughts and out of his kingdom as much as he could, he could not get away from Him. God was still ruling him and the kingdom of Israel. God continually sent prophets to Ahab to remind him of the Lord's will.

Part 3 — Ahab, the Thief

A man named Naboth had a vineyard next to King Ahab's palace in Jezreel. This land had come down to Naboth from his fathers, for you remember that by the law of Moses no man could sell his land. Each man's farm must always remain in his own family.

King Ahab wanted Naboth's land for a vegetable garden, because it was right next to his palace. He tried to buy it, offering to give Naboth a better vineyard for it; or, if Naboth should prefer, Ahab would pay for the field in money.

But Naboth would not sell it. He said, "The Lord forbids me to sell you the land which has come down to me from my fathers."

Ahab was very much displeased and disappointed. He went home, entered his bedroom, and lay down. He turned away his face, and would not come to dinner. The king of Israel sulked!

His wife Jezebel came to see what was the matter. She asked, "Why are you so sad, and why do you not come to dinner?"

Ahab responded, "Because I asked Naboth, our neighbor, to let me buy his vineyard, and he will not sell it to me."

Jezebel looked scornful. "Is that all that is the matter?" She asked. "Are you really king over Israel? Go and eat your dinner. I will give Naboth's vineyard to you."

Jezebel, having come from a heathen country, did not care for the law of Moses. She thought that the king ought to be able to take any land he wanted, whether the owner wished to sell it or not. The king should not have to ask!

Jezebel wrote letters to the elders of the city. She signed them with Ahab's name and sealed them with Ahab's seal. She wrote thus: "Proclaim a fast, and set Naboth at the head of the people. Bring two rough men before him. Tell them to say, 'Naboth cursed God and the king!' Of course then you must carry him out of the city and stone him to death."

The elders and the nobles were afraid to disobey Jezebel. They proclaimed a fast and set Naboth on high among the people. Two bad men, who had been hired for money, came in and said, "We heard Naboth curse God and the king."

As the law of Moses commanded, the people carried Naboth out of the city and stoned him till he was dead. Dogs licked his blood which stained the stones of that place.

Then word was sent to Jezebel that Naboth had been stoned and was dead. When Jezebel heard that news, she said to Ahab, "Arise and take possession of Naboth's vineyard which he would not sell you. He is not alive; he is dead."

The word of the Lord came to Elijah, saying: "Arise and go down to meet Ahab. He has gone to take Naboth's vineyard. Say to him, 'Thus saith the Lord: In the place where dogs licked the blood of Naboth, dogs shall lick your blood.'"

Elijah arose and strode sternly into the vineyard. Ahab, who was looking at the vines, realized that someone was behind him. He turned around. There stood the stern and frowning Elijah, whom the king had not seen for many years.

Ahab tremblingly gasped, "Have you found me, O my enemy?"

Elijah said, "I have found you, because you have sold yourself to do wickedness. God will punish you for this evil. He will take away all your sons. None of your family will be left, because you have made God angry. If your sons die in the city, the dogs will eat them; and if they die in the country, they will be eaten by vultures. The dogs will eat Jezebel by the wall of Jezreel."

There was never a king so wicked as Ahab, who did evil in the sight of the Lord, and who let himself be stirred up by his wicked wife. He worshipped idols, just as the heathen nations did, whom the Lord had cast out of Canaan.

Yet Ahab was an Israelite. He was not heathen, like his wife Jezebel. He knew that God rules the world, and he had seen God's power. After hearing Elijah's terrible words, he rent his clothes and put rough sackcloth on his bare skin. He ate no food and had no visitors.

The Lord said to Elijah, "Do you see that Ahab has humbled himself before Me? Because he has humbled himself, I will not bring this trouble upon his family in his lifetime; but in his son's days I will bring trouble upon his family."

CHAPTER 82

The Death of Ahab

I KINGS 22; II CHRONICLES 18

| *King of Israel* | *King of Judah* |
| Ahab | Jehoshaphat |

PART 1 — THE PROPHET WHO WOULD NOT LIE

What was happening in the kingdom of Judah while evil King Ahab was reigning in the kingdom of Israel?

After reigning for forty-one years, God-fearing King Asa died. He had a splendid funeral, for he was much beloved. Jehoshaphat, his son, was made king.

He too was a good king. The country prospered, and the people were happy.

Jehoshaphat made his country strong, especially on the northern border, where it joined the country of Israel. He made high walls around the border cities. He put soldiers in these cities and also in the towns of Ephraim which his father Asa had taken away from Israel.

The Lord helped Jehoshaphat in all that he did. The Lord was very much pleased with him, for he sought the Lord God as David had done. God made Jehoshaphat rich and prosperous.

When the nations around saw how the king of Judah prospered because he was true to his God, they were so much impressed that they too were inclined to fear and honor that God. None of those countries tried to make war on Jehoshaphat. Instead they brought him presents.

To make his country strong, Jehoshaphat built up a large army of more than a million trained soldiers, commanded by five captains.

This good king did another wise thing, even more important. He appointed men to teach the law of Moses to all the people. These teachers carried the book of the law with them.

Before this time the people had had little chance to learn the law, for books were so rare that only kings or very rich men could afford them. The books they did have were not printed, but were written with great care. Instead of paper, they were made of parchment, which is a fine white leather made from sheepskins.

If you could see one of these books you would hardly recognize what it was, for it would not look like the one which you are reading. These books were not made of many separate sheets. They were merely long strips of parchment with a stick at each end so that the strips could be rolled up, much as our window shades are rolled.

Although the good King Jehoshaphat took care that the people should learn about the law of God, he made a great mistake. He became friends with the wicked King Ahab, who had forgotten God.

With a great many servants and soldiers, Jehoshaphat made a visit to King Ahab. A splendid feast was given in his honor, to which all the nobles of the land were invited.

During the feast Ahab said to Jehoshaphat, "Do you not remember that the city of Ramoth in Gilead belongs to us, although the king of Syria has taken it away from us? We ought to go to war against the king of Syria, to get our city back again. Will you go with me?"

Jehoshaphat agreed with Ahab, but he would not go into any war without asking God about it first.

Ahab probably did not want Jehoshaphat to know that he did not worship God any longer; or perhaps he had gained a little faith since God had helped him in his last two wars. At any rate, he gathered together four hundred false prophets. These men were not prophets of Baal, nor were they true prophets of God. They were not prophets at all. They pretended that God spoke to them, but they made up their prophecies out of their own heads.

King Ahab said to these men, "Shall I go up to Ramoth-gilead to battle, or not?"

These men had received no word from God to give to the king. They wanted to speak so as to please him. So they said, "Go up, for the Lord will give you the city." Perhaps they thought that since God had helped them in the last war, He would help them in this one, too.

Jehoshaphat saw that they were not true prophets of God. He was not satisifed. "Haven't you a true prophet of God in your country?" he asked.

Ahab answered, "There is one prophet of God in my country, named Micaiah; but I hate him, for he never prophesies anything good for me, but always evil."

King Jehoshaphat answered, "Do not say that." He wanted a true message from God before he went to war.

Ahab sent a messenger to tell Micaiah to come quickly to him. The two kings sat on two thrones near the gate of Samaria, in a place where there were no houses. Before them stood the four hundred prophets, who kept saying, "Go up to Ramoth-gilead, for God will give it into your hands."

One of these false prophets had made two horns of iron. He came to the two kings and said, "Thus saith the Lord, 'With these horns you will push the Syrians till they are consumed.'" These words, like all the other prophecies, were a lie, for God had not spoken.

PART 2 — AHAB'S PLAN TO CHEAT DEATH

Should the two kings go to war to recover their city?

The messenger whom they sent found the true prophet Micaiah, and said, "All the four hundred prophets say nothing but good to the king. You must do as they do, and speak favorably."

Micaiah was a true prophet of God. He did not make up his prophecies just to please a wicked king. He was indignant with the messenger. "As the Lord lives," he said, "whatever the Lord tells me to say, that will I say."

With that determination, the prophet came before the two kings, who were sitting on their thrones with the four hundred false prophets in front of them. King Ahab asked at once, "Micaiah, shall I go and fight against Ramoth-gilead, or not?"

Micaiah answered very sarcastically, imitating the false prophets, "Go and prosper, for the Lord will deliver the city into your hand."

Ahab could tell from the tone of the prophet's voice that he was being mocked. He cried angrily, "How many times shall I warn you to speak nothing but the truth which God says to you?"

Then Micaiah threw up his arms, raised his face towards Heaven as if he saw a vision, and said, "I saw all Israel scattered upon the hills, as sheep that have no shepherd, and the Lord said, 'These have no master. Let them go to their homes.'"

Of course, this vision meant that Ahab would be killed if he went into the battle, and the Israelites would have no king. Ahab turned to Jehoshaphat and exclaimed, "Did I not tell you that he would prophesy no good for me, but only evil?"

But Micaiah was not yet through. Again he held up his arms, raising his eyes as if he saw a vision. In a commanding voice he went on:

"I saw the Lord sitting on His throne, surrounded by all the host of Heaven. The Lord said, 'Who will persuade Ahab to go up to Ramoth-gilead and be killed?'

"One spirit said one thing, and another spirit said something else. At last a spirit came and stood before the Lord and said, 'I will go and persuade Ahab.' The Lord asked 'How will you persuade him?' The spirit answered, 'I will be a lying spirit in the mouths of all King Ahab's prophets.'

"Now listen, King Ahab. God has put a lying spirit into the mouths of all your prophets. What they have said is not true. The

Lord has told me that if you go up to Ramoth-gilead, you will die there."

Did King Ahab give up going to Ramoth-gilead? No. In spite of this harsh prophecy, King Ahab was determined to have his own way. He had beaten the Syrians twice before, and he believed that he could do it again. He had forgotten that it was not by his own might, but by the help of the Lord, that he had won those other victories.

For many years Ahab had lived like a heathen, never thinking of God nor trying to obey Him. Now when God sent him this message by Micaiah, it did not mean much to Ahab. Four hundred prophets told him to go to Ramoth-gilead, and only this one told him not to go. He wanted to do what the four hundred advised.

Ahab decided to punish Micaiah for giving a disagreeable prophecy. He called some soldiers and said, "Put Micaiah in prison and feed him with prison bread and bad prison water till I come back from this war. I shall come back soon in peace, and he will see that his prophecy did not come true."

The two kings went to Ramoth-gilead. Instead of putting on his handsome kingly robes, Ahab dressed just like a common soldier. He thought that if no one should know who he was, he would not be killed.

But Ahab told Jehoshaphat, the king of Judah, to wear all his royal robes. Probably Ahab thought in his heart that the enemy might take Jehoshaphat for the king of Israel, and kill him.

The king of Syria had thirty-two captains over his soldiers. All these captains were commanded not to fight with common soldiers, but to try to kill the king of Israel.

When these men saw King Jehoshaphat dressed in kingly robes, they thought he was the man they were looking for. They surrounded him to capture and kill him, but Jehoshaphat cried out in terror, "I am not the king of Israel!" The captains soon were convinced of this fact, and left him alone.

It so happened that a soldier in the Syrian army drew his bow and shot into the air aimlessly. That arrow flew straight to King Ahab and entered the tiny hole where his armor was fastened together.

Ahab said faintly to the driver of his chariot, "Turn around and drive me out of the battle, for I am wounded."

The wounded king lay in a pool of his own blood at the bottom of his chariot. The fierce battle went on, while Ahab bled to death. At evening he died. His men took his body to Samaria, where he was buried.

Ahab's servants took the chariot to the pool of Samaria to wash it. There the wild dogs of the city licked up the blood of King Ahab in the place where Naboth had been stoned.

So the prophecy that Elijah had spoken came true.

CHAPTER 83

God Protects His People

II Kings 1; II Chronicles 20, 21

King of Israel	Kings of Judah
Ahaziah	Jehoshaphat
	Jehoram

PART 1 — FIRE FROM HEAVEN WHICH SAVED ELIJAH

Ahab was dead, but his wife Jezebel was still living. Their son, Ahaziah, was now king in Israel. Like his father and mother, this king was wicked. He did not worship God, but worshiped the heathen idol Baal.

Ahaziah was king for only two years. He fell out of an upstairs window in his palace, and was hurt very badly. He wanted to know whether he would get better or would die. He never thought of asking God, for he had been taught as a child to worship idols. He sent messages to one of the cities of the Philistines, where there was a heathen idol named Baal-zebub, to ask whether he would get well or not.

God was angry with Ahaziah. Before the messengers had gone far on their journey, they were met by an austere old man. It was the prophet Elijah, sent by God with a message. He strode up to the men and demanded, "Why do you go to inquire to Baal-zebub? Go back to your master and say to him, 'Have you sent to Baal-zebub because there is no God in Israel? You shall surely die as a punishment for worshipping idols.' "

The messengers turned around and went back to the sick king.

"Why have you come back?" he asked.

They replied, "There came a man to meet us. He commanded us to come back again to the king who sent us and say, 'Is it because there is no God in Israel that you are sending to inquire of the idol Baalzebub whether you will die or get well? Because you have done this, you will not get well, but will surely die.'"

When the sick king heard these dreadful words, he had a suspicion that the prophet might be the terrible Elijah who had come so many times to his father with warnings of woe. If it were Elijah, he knew that he would surely die, for Elijah's prophecies always came true.

"What kind of man was he?" he asked.

"He was a hairy man, wearing a leather belt," was the answer.

King Ahaziah knew that the strange man must have been Elijah. As Jezebel had done, he tried to kill the prophet. He sent a captain with fifty soldiers to find Elijah and bring him to the palace, so that Ahaziah could punish him for his bad news.

The captain of the fifty soldiers found Elijah sitting on the top of a hill. He called out, "Man of God, the king has said, 'Come down!'"

Elijah knew very well that the king meant to kill him, just as Jezebel had tried many times. He said to the captain, "If I am a man of God, God will take care of me by sending fire down from Heaven to burn up you and your fifty soldiers."

Before the terrified man could do anything, God sent fire down from Heaven which burned up the king's soldiers.

Did Ahaziah, when he heard this news, bow before the mighty God? No, he would not acknowledge God's power. If he had been a Hittite or a Philistine, this would not have been so strange; but he was an Israelite on his father's side.

Ahaziah sent another captain with fifty other soldiers to bring Elijah to be tortured and killed. The second captain came to Elijah with his fifty soldiers behind him. He, too, commanded, "O man of God, the king says, 'Come down at once.'"

Elijah said, "If I am a man of God, let fire come down from Heaven and burn you and your fifty soldiers."

Again God protected His faithful prophet, who dared to stand up for the Lord and to reprove a sinful king, even at the risk of his own life. A second time God sent down fire from Heaven.

Ahaziah did not yield. He sent a third captain with fifty other soldiers after Elijah. But this captain feared the God of the Israelites, even though the king did not. When he came near to Elijah, he fell down on his knees and begged the prophet to save his life and the lives of his fifty soldiers.

God told Elijah to go with this man. So Elijah went to see the sick king. He entered the bedroom and boldly said to the king,

"Because you have sent to ask the idol whether you will get well, instead of sending to the God of Israel, therefore you will never be able to leave your bed again. You will soon die."

In a short time the word of Elijah was fulfilled. King Ahaziah died. As he had no son, his brother Joram, who is sometimes called Jehoram in the Bible, became king.

Part 2 — A Victory Without a Battle

After the death of Ahab, King Jehoshaphat returned to his own country. He went throughout the land, urging the people to worship the Lord. He appointed judges in all the important cities, warning them to be just, since they were judging for God and not for man.

After a time some messengers came to Jehoshaphat and said, "A great army of Moabites and Ammonites and Edomites is coming to fight against you. They have already come as far as En-gedi."

This was the wild rocky country west of the Dead Sea, called "the rocks of the wild goats," where David hid from Saul.

Jehoshaphat began to pray to the Lord for help. He proclaimed a fast-day throughout all the cities of Judah. The people of the land came to Jerusalem and stood before the Temple — the women and children as well as the men. The king stood in the court of the Temple and raised his arms and his face to Heaven, and prayed to God.

God had driven out the people of Canaan before His people, and had given the land to the Israelites forever. He had promised that if evil should come upon them, if they would stand before the Temple and cry unto Him in their trouble, then He would hear and help them. Now great trouble had come upon them. Jehoshaphat prayed for God's help, for he knew his people could never conquer the army that approached, unless God would be with them.

While the people were praying, the Spirit of the Lord came upon a Levite. God told him to say that the people should go out against their enemies, but the Lord would do all the fighting for them.

King Jehoshaphat dropped down on his knees and bowed his head. The host of the people worshipped the Lord, while some of the priests stood up to sing.

The next morning the people rose early and went into the wilderness to meet the army that was coming against them. In front marched a large choir, praising God in songs as they went.

In the great host of people who had come to make war against the Israelites there were three nations: the Moabites, the Ammonites, and the Edomites. As the children of Israel began to sing, the Lord made the Moabites and the Ammonites to fight against the Edomites. After they had destroyed the Edomites, they began to kill each other.

There was a watch-tower in the wilderness. As soon as the Israelites reached it, they climbed up to see where the enemy was. To their unspeakable surprise, the whole country was covered with dead bodies. Not a living man could be seen!

The children of Israel found a great abundance of riches and precious jewels. It took them three days to carry away all the riches that they found.

On the fourth day they came together and thanked the Lord for the marvelous thing He had done for them. Not only had their enemies been destroyed, but they themselves were going back much richer than they had come out. With King Jehoshaphat at the head, the Israelites marched back to Jerusalem in a joyful procession, accompanied by the triumphant shrilling of trumpets, and the sweet sound of harps and psalteries.

Of course, the news of the wonderful victory of the children of Judah was heard in every country round about. All the heathen nations were afraid when they heard how the Lord fought against the enemies of Israel. God gave the land peace.

Jehoshaphat reigned over Judah twenty-five years. He was like his father Asa, doing what was right in the eyes of the Lord. At last his time came to die. He slept with his fathers, and was buried with them in the city of David. His son Jehoram reigned in his stead.

Sad to say, Jehoram was a very bad man and a very bad king. As soon as he became king, he killed his six brothers and some of the princes of Judah, so that they would not try to take the kingdom away from him.

Why did King Jehoram copy wicked Ahab instead of his father, good King Jehoshaphat? Because he had Ahab's daughter for his wife.

You remember that Jehoshaphat had once paid a visit to King Ahab. He had taken his young son with him on that visit. Jehoram had fallen in love with Ahab's pretty daughter, Athaliah. He did not know that she was just as bad a woman as her mother. He married her and brought her back to Jerusalem.

Just as wicked Queen Jezebel had influenced King Ahab, so Athaliah influenced Jehoram. He became an idolater. What was worse, he forced the people of Judah to idol-worship.

The old prophet Elijah, who had so many times warned King Ahab, sent a letter to King Jehoram, warning him that God would punish him.

Because Jehoram worshipped idols, God permitted the surrounding nations to make trouble for him. The Philistines and the Arabians forced their way into the land. They came into Jerusalem, even into the king's palace. They stole all the fine things they found. They took away Jehoram's wives and sons, so that only his youngest son was left.

Jehoram finally became ill. After two years of suffering, he died. No one was sorry at his death, for he had been a bad ruler. He was buried in Jerusalem, but not in the graves of the kings.

CHAPTER 84

Good-bye to Elijah

II KINGS 2

King of Israel	King of Judah
Joram	Jehoram

We must leave the kings of Israel and Judah for a while. The time has come for us to say good-bye to the great prophet Elijah.

Elijah lived in evil days. In his lifetime King Ahab had been on the throne of Israel, and after him his wicked son Ahaziah. Still more wicked than either was the idolatrous Queen Jezebel. Ahab and Jezebel had turned the hearts of the people of Israel away, so that God was forgotten except by a faithful few.

It had been Elijah's mission to tell these idolatrous kings of God's terrible punishment for their sins. The kings had hated him and tried to kill him. Only God's care had saved his life.

It was no wonder that wicked kings feared and hated the stern prophet. He always came to announce some dire punishment for their wickedness and idolatry. They had tried over and over to kill him instead of changing their ways.

At last Elijah's work was over. God was going to take him to Heaven. Elijah and Elisha were living at Gilgal when the word of the Lord came, telling Elijah to depart. "Stay here," the old prophet said to Elisha, "for the Lord has sent me to Bethel."

But Elisha did not want to part from Elijah. "As the Lord lives," he said, "I will not leave you."

Together they went to Bethel, where there was a school of the prophets. The prophets came out to meet Elisha, asking, "Do you know that God is going to take your master away today?"

Elisha replied, "Yes, I know it. You need not tell me."

Again Elijah said to his follower, "Stay here, for the Lord has sent me to Jericho."

But Elisha said, as before, "As the Lord lives and as your soul lives, I will not leave you."

At Jericho there was another school of the prophets. These prophets, too, came to Elisha and asked him, "Do you know that God is going to take away your master today?"

"Yes, I know it," he answered. "You need not tell me."

Elijah suggested to Elisha, "You had better stay here. The Lord has sent me to the Jordan."

But Elisha wanted to see his teacher go to Heaven. So he said again, "As surely as the Lord lives and your soul lives, I will not leave you."

The prophets knew that something wonderful was going to happen. They too were eager to see what God was going to do for Elijah. They went to a high place where they could watch what would happen.

When Elijah and Elisha came to the River Jordan, Elijah took his mantle and wrapped it together. He struck the waters with it, and the waters were divided, so that Elijah and Elisha walked through the river on dry ground.

On the other side of the Jordan, Elijah asked Elisha, "Is there anything you would like to have me do for you, before I am taken away from you?"

Elisha said, "I would like to ask that a double portion of your spirit may fall on me."

"You have asked a hard thing, but if you see me when I am taken away from you, you shall have it," Elijah answered.

The two men walked on together. As they were walking and talking, a most marvelous thing happened. There appeared out of the sky a chariot of fire and horses of fire, which came down from Heaven to carry Elijah to God.

Elijah climbed into the chariot. The horses and the chariot flew in a whirlwind up into Heaven. As Elisha saw him go, he cried out, "My father, my father, the chariots of Israel and the horsemen!"

He watched and watched, until the chariot disappeared in the blue of the sky. Elijah's mantle dropped off and fell at Elisha's feet. Elisha took up the mantle and went back to the bank of the Jordan. He wrapped the mantle together and struck the water with it, saying, "Where is the Lord God of Elijah?"

The waters divided, just as they had done for his teacher, showing God had chosen him to take Elijah's place.

The young men from the school of the prophets, who had been watching from a distance, came to meet Elisha. They bowed before him, for they saw that the spirit of Elijah was resting on him.

They said to him, "Perhaps the Spirit of the Lord may have taken Elijah to some mountain or valley and dropped him there. There are fifty strong men with us. Let us go and hunt for him."

Elisha refused, for he knew that Elijah had gone to Heaven. The young prophets, however, kept on begging him to let them see if they could not find Elijah in some lonely valley or on some rugged mountain peak. At last Elisha said, "Go," although he knew it was of no use.

The fifty men searched the mountains and valleys for three days. They could not find Elijah, of course. At last they had to believe that God had taken Elijah directly from earth to Heaven, as He had taken Enoch so many years before.

After this, Elisha went back to Bethel, where he lived. On the way, he passed through Jericho. In this city there lived a great many rude, naughty boys. These boys ran after the prophet, and called him names, pointing their fingers at him and saying mockingly, "Go up, you baldhead! Go up, you baldhead!"

They were doing wrong, for God has commanded children to respect old people. Elisha turned and cursed them in the name of the Lord.

God sent two bears, which ran after those boys and killed forty-two of them. This was a punishment for disobeying God's special command to children that they should be respectful to old people.

CHAPTER 85

Elisha, the Gentle Prophet

II KINGS 4, 5

King of Israel	*King of Judah*
Joram	Jehoram

PART 1 — TWO BOYS SAVED FROM SLAVERY

Like Elijah, Elisha was a prophet of God. But he was a very different sort of man, and he had a very different sort of work to do. He was not like the stern Elijah, nor was he sent to reprove kings.

Let us go back a little over the story of Judah and Israel. King Ahaziah of Israel, you remember, fell out of a window and sent to an idol god to find out whether he would get well. God was angry with him and gave him only two years as king.

Since Ahaziah had no son to rule after him, his brother Joram became king over Israel. Joram was not a good man, but he was not so bad as his father Ahab and his brother.

Good King Jehoshaphat, an old man, was still reigning in Judah when Joram became king of Israel. His son Jehoram, who became the next king, was not God-fearing. He worshipped idols as Ahab had done, because he had married Ahab's daughter. God punished him with sickness and war.

It was in the days of these kings that Elisha lived. He worked among the people, teaching and helping them.

One day a woman came to him for help. Her husband had been one of the sons of the prophets. He was dead, and the woman was so poor that she could hardly get enough to eat.

This widow had a debt which she was too poor to pay. One day the man to whom she owed the money came to her house to take away her two sons, to make them slaves. This was the custom in that time: when one had no money to pay his debts, his children were taken as slaves.

The poor woman did not know what to do. In her trouble she came to Elisha.

The prophet inquired, "What have you in your house?"

"I haven't anything except a pot of olive oil," she answered.

Elisha said, "Go and borrow from your neighbors all the jars that you can find. Shut the door, so that no one can come in. Pour oil from your pot into all those jars."

The woman sent her sons to all the neighbors to borrow pots and vessels. Then she shut the door. She poured olive oil into the jars as the boys brought them to her. God made her oil increase so much that there was enough to fill all the borrowed jars.

When she had filled every one, the oil in her own jar stopped running. Then she went to Elisha. He told her to go and sell the oil and pay her debt. She and her sons might live on the money that would be left over.

So Elisha helped one poor woman.

PART 2 — HOW A DEAD CHILD BECAME ALIVE

There was a rich woman living in Shunem, a town which Elisha often visited.

As often as the prophet came to Shunem, this lady invited him to come to her house for supper. She became well acquainted with him. One day she said to her husband, "Let us build a little room upstairs for this holy man who comes this way so often. Let us put a bed in it, and a table, and a chair, and a light, so that he can stay all night whenever he pleases."

Elisha was very much pleased with the kindness of this good woman. One day while he was at her home, he said to his servant Gehazi, "Call this lady to come here."

When the lady had come in, Elisha said, "It was very good of you to do all this for me. Now I would like to return your kindness, and do something for you. What shall I do for you? Shall I speak to the king for you, or to the captain of the army?"

She said, "No, thank you. I do not want **anything**."

When she had gone, Elisha asked his servant **Gehazi**, "What **can** I do for her?"

Gehazi knew by this time that Elisha could do wonderful **things**, by the power of God. So he said to Elisha. "She **has no child, and her** husband is an old man."

Elisha called the woman back again and **said to her, "Next year** you shall have a baby boy."

Oh, how delighted the lady was! She had never had a baby, although she had wanted one more than anything else in the world. She could hardly believe Elisha. All that year she began to get ready for the darling baby that Elisha had said was coming to her. How happy she was as she sat sewing on the tiny baby clothes she was making for him!

The next year the baby came. Oh, how she loved him. How happy she was when she rocked him to sleep in her arms!

By and by, he grew up to be a sturdy little boy. When he was **five** or six years old, he went out one day to his father's farm to see the reapers gather the wheat. It was a hot summer day. The sun poured down on the harvest field. In the heat, the little boy got a sunstroke. He cried to his father, "My head! My head!"

"Carry him to his mother," commanded his father to one of **his** servants.

The little boy was carried back to the house. His mother did all she could for him. She held him in her lap and put cool water on **his** head, but he got worse and worse. About noon, he died.

His mother carried him upstairs to Elisha's room and laid him **on** the bed. Then she went to her husband and said, "Send me one **of** the young men and an ass, for I want to go to see Elisha as soon **as** possible." The servant brought an ass, and she saddled it. "Drive just as fast as you can," she urged.

Solomon was very rich and highly honoured. 1 Kings 10

There appeared out of the sky a chariot of fire and horses of fire.

2 Kings 2

The man of God saw the lady coming along the road, far off. He commanded Gehazi to meet her and ask her if she and her husband and her child were well.

Elisha's servant ran to meet the lady. She did not want to tell all her trouble to Gehazi; so she answered, "It is well," and hurried on. When she reached Elisha's house on the hill and saw the good man who had been her friend, she threw herself on the ground in front of him and burst into tears.

Gehazi was going to push her away, but Elisha said, "Let her alone. She is in trouble."

Between her sobs, the lady managed to say, "Did I ask for a son?"

Elisha said to Gehazi, "Run quickly to the lady's house. Do not stop to talk to anyone on the way. Lay my staff on the face of the child."

Gehazi tucked his long robe into his belt, so that it would not get in his way as he ran. Elisha himself followed with the lady.

Gehazi laid Elisha's staff on the face of the child, but it did no good. He ran back to meet Elisha and said, "The child did not awaken."

When Elisha reached the lady's house, he went up into his own little room, where the child lay upon the bed. Elisha lay down upon the bed over the child. He put his mouth on the little boy's mouth, his eyes over the boy's eyes, and his hands upon the child's hands. The dead body of the little boy became warm.

Then Elisha got up and walked about a little. Again he stretched himself upon the child. The boy sneezed seven times and opened his eyes. Elisha called his servant and told him to bring the lady.

The dear little boy lay on the bed with the rosy color of health on his cheeks. When he looked up and stretched out his arms, the mother was overcome with joy. She first fell down at Elisha's feet in thanks. Then she took up her little son and carried him down to his own room.

PART 3 — THE GENERAL WHO OBEYED ORDERS

To the north of Israel lay the land of Syria, where Ben-hadad ruled. This man had been king for many, many years, and had often made war against Israel. Twice he and the Syrian Army had been defeated by the Israelites under Ahab. In another war between the two countries Ahab had been killed.

But when Joram became king of Israel, there was peace with Ben-hadad. Although at times the Syrians came in bands and stole the property of the Israelites, there were no wars.

The captain of the armies of Ben-hadad was a man named Naaman. He was a great favorite with his master. God had helped Naaman to conquer many of Syria's enemies. In spite of this, the general had that most terrible of all diseases, leprosy.

Some time before our story begins, a band of Syrians had gone down into the northern part of the land of Israel, and had stolen away a little girl. She became a servant in Naaman's house, to wait upon his wife. Since they were kind to the little girl, she loved her master and mistress.

One day she happened to say to her mistress, "Oh, how I wish that my lord Naaman were in Samaria, for there is a prophet there who would cure him of his leprosy."

The words of the little girl came to the king. They caused a great sensation in the court, for no one had ever before heard of anyone who could cure leprosy. Ben-hadad finally said to his general Naaman, "If it is true that there is a prophet in Samaria who can cure you of your leprosy, you must go down there and see him. I will give you a letter of introduction to King Joram."

So Naaman went to Samaria. He took a fine present with him — more than forty-eight thousand dollars' worth of gold and silver, and ten beautiful silken robes.

He did not go to Elisha, for he did not know where the prophet lived. He went to the king of Israel and gave him Ben-hadad's letter. This is what the message said: "With this letter I have sent my general Naaman to you, so that you can cure him of his leprosy."

King Ben-hadad supposed that if King Joram had a wonderful prophet who could cure leprosy, this prophet would be living at the king's court.

But King Joram did not know very much about Elisha. He was frightened when he got this letter. He could not understand why King Ben-hadad should send Naaman to him. *He* could not cure an incurable disease. He thought King Ben-hadad was just trying to pick a quarrel with him. King Joram tore his clothes in his dismay.

All the people of Samaria heard about the letter which their king had received from Ben-hadad, the king of Syria. Elisha also heard about Naaman's coming to the king of Israel to be cured of leprosy. He sent a messenger to Joram to say, "Let the general come to me, and he will find out that there is a prophet in Israel."

In fine style, with his handsome horses and his grand chariot, Naaman drove to Elisha's house. The prophet did not come out to meet Naaman. He only sent a messenger to say to him, "Go and wash in the Jordan River seven times, and you will be cured. The leprosy will leave you, and your flesh will become fresh and healthy."

Naaman was an important man. He was rich and honored. Never in his life had he been given such cool treatment. He left Elisha's house angrily, saying, "I thought he would surely come out to me, and call on the name of the Lord his God, waving his hand over the place to make me well again. The idea of sending a messenger to me and telling me to go and wash in the Jordan! Are not the rivers of Damascus better than all the waters of Israel? I can just as well go home and wash in my own rivers."

Naaman's servants felt sorry that he was angry, for he was a kind master. They loved him and wanted him to get well. They tried to talk him out of his bad mood, saying, "My father, if the prophet had told you to do some very hard thing, would you not have done it? Then why not do this little thing that he tells you to do? He only said, 'Wash, and you will be well.'"

Naaman finally gave in. He ordered the driver of his chariot to go down to the Jordan. Naaman took off his clothes and waded into the river, dipping himself into it seven times.

Then he looked at his body. The leprosy was all gone! His skin instead of being deadly white, was as pink and rosy as a little child's.

Naaman felt that this unbelievable cure was worked by Elisha's God. He had heard many stories of the power of the God of the Israelites. Now he felt sure that Jehovah was the only true God.

He and all his servants turned back to Elisha's house. Naaman said to the prophet, "Now I know there is no God in all the earth, except in Israel. Let me give you the gift which I have brought with me."

Elisha refused. He did not want any pay for what the Lord had done. He wanted Naaman to understand that it was the Lord who had cured him.

Naaman did understand this. He promised never to offer sacrifice or burnt offering to any god except Jehovah. "I will still have to go with my master into the temple of the idol Rimmon," he said. "May the Lord forgive me for that, for I will bow only with my head, not with my heart. In my heart I know that there is only one God in all the earth. I would like to have two mules' burden of earth from Samaria to take with me, so that when I worship the Lord, I can kneel on holy earth."

At last the great soldier said good-bye to Elisha, and the prophet answered "Go in peace."

Now, Gehazi, Elisha's servant, said to himself, "What a pity it is that my master did not take the gift Naaman offered him! I will run after him and ask him for some of those fine things."

Gehazi ran after the Syrian. When Naaman saw Elisha's servant hurrying after him, he stopped his chariot, thinking that Elisha had sent after him. He asked, "Is all well?"

Gehazi said, "Yes, all is well. But just now there came to see us two young men who are sons of the prophets. My master sent me after you to ask you to give them a talent of silver and two robes as a present."

Naaman was glad to do this. He urged, "One talent is not enough. Take two." He gave Gehazi two bags filled with silver and two suits of beautiful silken clothes. How much money do you think there was in those two bags? There was more than three thousand dollars in them! Naaman had to send two of his servants with Gehazi to carry the money.

Gehazi did not let them carry those bags back to Elisha's house. No indeed! He stopped them when they came to a tower. There he hid the money in a secret place.

He let the two servants of Naaman return to their master. He himself went on to Elisha's house, as though nothing had happened.

"Where have you been, Gehazi?" asked the prophet.

"I have been nowhere," answered the servant.

Elisha said, "Did not my heart go with you, when Naaman stopped his chariot to meet you? Is it right for you to receive these gifts? For this, the leprosy of Naaman shall come upon you and your children."

Gehazi went out of the room. He was a leper! His flesh was as white as snow.

CHAPTER 86

Trouble with Syria

II KINGS 6, 7, 8

King of Israel	*Kings of Judah*
Joram	Jehoram
	Ahaziah

PART 1 — ELISHA FOOLS THE SYRIANS

Again there was war between Syria and Israel. As you remember, when Ahab was king, the Syrians fought against the Israelites near the hill of Samaria and when they were defeated, they thought it was because Jehovah was a god of the hills. The next year they fought in the valleys, for they thought the God of Israel was not a god of the valleys. For that very reason, God gave the Israelites the victory; He wanted the Syrians to learn that Jehovah is the God of the whole earth.

Since Ahab had had two victories, he thought he could conquer the Syrians again. He persuaded Jehoshaphat to go with him to war against the Syrians. The prophet Micaiah warned him that he would lose his life in the battle, but Ahab paid no attention to the warning. He was killed by a stray arrow.

Since then, there had been peace with Syria. But now Ben-hadad, the king of Syria, again planned to go to war against Israel.

The Syrians chose carefully the place where they wanted to fight. When they had set up their camp there, Elisha sent word to King Joram not to go near the place where the Syrian army was secretly camped. So Joram saved himself from the Syrians.

This happened two or three times. Ben-hadad could not understand why the king of Israel never came near his camp. He thought that there must be a traitor in his army who told the king of Israel where his camp was so that he might avoid it.

He said to his soldiers, "I want you to tell me who is going to the king of Israel and telling him all about my plans."

One of his servants said, "My lord, O king, no one is doing that. Elisha, the prophet that is in Israel, tells the king of Israel the words that you speak in your bedroom."

King Ben-hadad commanded, "Go and find out where he is, so that I can send and catch him."

The men came back, saying, "He is in Dothan."

Ben-hadad sent horses and chariots and a host of soldiers to Dothan, where Elisha was living. They came at night and surrounded the city.

Early in the morning, Elisha's servant went outdoors. He was terrified to see that the whole city was surrounded by horses and chariots. He hurried into the house to tell Elisha, crying out, "Alas, my master, what shall we do?"

But Elisha was not afraid, for he could see something that his servant could not see. "Do not be afraid," said he. "We have more to help us than they have." Then Elisha prayed to the Lord to open the eyes of his servant so that he might see. God opened his eyes. What do you suppose he saw? God had sent horses and chariots of fire from Heaven to take care of Elisha.

When Ben-hadad's soldiers came close to Elisha, the prophet prayed to the Lord to make them all blind, so that they could not see. He said to them, "You have made a mistake. This is not the way, nor is this the right city. Follow me, and I will bring you to the man you are looking for."

He led them into the capital city of Samaria. When they were in the middle of the city, Elisha said, "Lord, open the eyes of these men, so that they may see where they are." The Lord opened their eyes, and they saw that they were in the middle of Samaria, the city of their enemies!

King Joram was very much excited. Here were the enemies trapped in his biggest city, where he could easily kill them! He called out to Elisha, "My father, shall I kill them? Shall I kill them?"

But Elisha said, "No, no, that would not be right. Give them some bread to eat, and some water to drink, and let them go home to their master."

Instead of killing the Syrians, King Joram gave them good food. Then he sent them home.

PART 2 — A CITY ESCAPES STARVATION

For a time, the Syrians were ashamed to come again to the land of Israel to steal and kill. But peace did not last. Ben-hadad came again in earnest to fight against Samaria.

With him he brought a great host of soldiers. They surrounded the city of Samaria, so that none of the people of the city could go out or come in. There is nothing more dreadful than such a siege. It means slow starvation for the people inside the city walls.

Before long, all the food in the city of Samaria was eaten up. The starving people could get no more food from the farmers outside, because the Syrian soldiers would let no one into Samaria. The little food that was left in the city was so expensive, that poor people could not buy it. They killed every animal that was in the city and ate it — even animals that were not fit to eat. Even those were very, very expensive. The head of a donkey cost eighty pieces of silver.

King Joram took a walk on the wall of the city. On every side he could see people in distress, suffering from starvation. He thought that Elisha was to blame for this siege, and he made up his mind to kill the prophet that very day.

He sent a messenger to Elisha, who sat in his house with the elders of Israel. Elisha knew the messenger was coming. He shut the door and would not let him in.

The king himself followed his messenger. Elisha said to the king, "God says that tomorrow about this time, a measure of fine flour shall be sold for a shekel, and two measures of barley for a shekel."

A shekel was a small piece of money, worth about fifty cents. A man standing near the king, on whose arm the king leaned, did not believe Elisha's message. He spoke very scornfully, "Even if the Lord should make windows in Heaven, could this be true?"

"You shall see it with your own eyes," Elisha answered, "but you shall not eat any of it."

On this same day four poor lepers sat by the gate of the city. They said to each other, "Why should we sit here until we die? If we go into the city, we shall surely die from the famine. If we stay here, we shall die here too. Let us go down to the camp of the Syrians. If they save us alive, we shall live; and if they kill us we shall meet nothing worse than death."

They thought that because they were lepers, the Syrians might be afraid to touch them. Perhaps they could pick up some few crusts of stale bread that the soldiers had thrown into the garbage heaps.

The lepers rose up in the evening to go into the camp of the Syrians. To their great surprise, they found the camp empty! They went from one tent to another, throughout the camp. Not a soul was there! The Syrians had gone, leaving everything behind.

What had happened was this: The Lord had made the Syrians hear a noise that sounded like the tramp of horses and the rattle of the chariots of a great host of soldiers. The Syrians had said to one another in terror, "What is that? It must be that the king of Israel has hired other kings to come against us. Oh, hurry! Let us run, or we shall be killed!" In their terror, they had left their tents and their horses and everything else just as it was, and had run for their lives.

The four lepers went through all the tents. When they found that all the tents were empty, they ate and drank till they were satisfied. Then they took gold, silver, and fine clothes and hid them.

At last they said to each other. "We are not doing right. This is a day of good news. We ought to go and tell the king. We shall surely be punished if we selfishly keep this to ourselves."

It was night by the time they returned to the city. The city gate was shut tight, locked and barred, because of the Syrians. The lepers stood outside the gate and shouted to the porter, "We came to the camp of the Syrians, and there was no one there. All was as still as death. The horses and asses were tied and the tents were not taken down."

The porter of the gate called some other men. They went to the king's palace in the middle of the night. The king's servants came in answer to their knock. They awakened the king to tell him the wonderful news.

The king did not believe that it was true. He said, "I shall tell you what the Syrians have done. They know that we are hungry, and they have only pretended to go away. They have gone out into the fields and hid themselves, planning to catch us alive and get into the city."

But some of King Joram's servants said, "Let us take five of the horses that are left, and see if the good news can possibly be true."

These men went out to the camp of the Syrians. They found that the news brought by the lepers was true. There was no one in the camp. Then the king's servants went on till they came to the Jordan River. All the road was strewn with garments and kettles and other things that the Syrians had flung away in their hurry. There was no sign of any Syrian soldier anywhere.

It was some time before the people believed that it was safe to go outside the city. Finally the starving Israelites poured out of the city in crowds to the camp of the Syrians. They were frantic to get food. They came in such a rush, that many people were knocked down and hurt.

The king appointed the lord on whose arm he leaned to have charge of the gate. The people crowded and pushed so, that the lord was knocked down and trodden under foot by the wild rush of people.

Before he died, he saw Elisha's prophecy fulfilled. The people who got to the camp first, after they had satisfied their hunger, took bags of flour and meal. Standing near the gate, they sold food to the late comers, who had just reached the gate.

As Elisha had said, the man who had doubted his word saw two measures of barley sold for a shekel, but could not eat of it.

Part 3 — A Thought Which Became a Murder

Do you remember that when the Lord appeared to Elijah in the still small voice on Mount Sinai, He told the prophet to go back and anoint a new king over Syria, and a new king over Israel? Elijah did not accomplish this work in his lifetime. He passed it on to Elisha.

Elisha went up to Damascus in Syria. Ben-hadad, the king, was sick. He was now an old man, for he had reigned a long time.

Ben-hadad was heathen, and he worshipped the idol Rimmon. Even after his great general Naaman had been cured of leprosy, he did not become a worshipper of God. He must have learned something of the greatness of the God of Israel, however. When his servants told him that Elisha, the man of God, had come to Damascus,

Ben-hadad said to his servant Hazael, "Take a present, and go and meet the man of God. Ask him to inquire of God whether I will get well of this disease, or not."

Hazael went to meet Elisha. He spoke very respectfully. "Your son, Ben-hadad, king of Syria, has sent me to you to ask you whether he will get well of this disease."

Elisha said to the king's servant, "Go tell him that he will get well of this sickness." Looking very earnestly at Hazael, Elisha continued in a low tone, "But the Lord has showed me that he will surely die."

Hazael was very much puzzled by this strange message. He was still more perplexed when he saw that Elisha was looking at him very earnestly and solemnly. Great tears rolled down Elisha's cheeks.

Hazael asked, "Why do you weep, my lord?"

"Because I know all the dreadful things that you are going to do to the children of Israel. You will burn their cities. You will kill their young men with the sword. You will dash their little ones to death on stones."

Hazael was horrified. Why did Elisha say such things to him? He would surely never do such terrible things. He protested to Elisha, "What do you mean? Who do you think I am, that I should act in this brutal way?"

Elisha gave an answer that astonished Hazael. "The Lord has showed me that you are to be the king of Syria."

You can imagine Hazael's feelings. What! Was he to be the king of Syria when Ben-hadad died? He kept thinking about it all the way home to the palace.

When King Ben-hadad asked him what the prophet had told him, he said, "The prophet said that you will surely get well." But he did not tell Ben-hadad the rest that Elisha had said.

All night long Hazael could not sleep. He kept thinking of what Elisha had said — that he should be king after Ben-hadad. How fine that would be! But he would have to wait a long time, for Elisha had said that Ben-hadad would get well. Hazael almost wished that Elisha had said that Ben-hadad would die of his sickness. Then Hazael could be king immediately.

The more he thought about it, the more Hazael wished that the king would die. At last the sinful thought came into his heart, that it would be very easy to make Ben-hadad die. He was old and sick. It would be easy to smother him.

All night long Hazael made his plans. The next morning he took a thick cloth, dipped it in water, and spread it over Ben-hadad's face, holding it down so tight that Ben-hadad could not breathe.

The weak, sick old man struggled a little, but soon his struggles stopped. He was dead. Probably the people never knew that Hazael had murdered the king. They thought that he had died naturally, of his sickness. But Elisha knew the truth, and Hazael knew.

The new king, who had begun his reign by murdering his master, became a cruel and bloody king. In the course of time, he did all the wicked things that Elisha had foretold.

CHAPTER 87

The Soldier-King, Jehu

II Chronicles 21, 22; II Kings 9, 10

Kings of Israel	*King of Judah*
Joram	Ahaziah
Jehu	

Part 1 — A Secret Anointing

We have not heard about the kingdom of Judah for a long time. The last thing we learned about it was that Jehoram became king after the death of good King Jehoshaphat, his father.

Jehoram was not a good king as his father had been. He had married a wicked wife — Athaliah, the daughter of Ahab and Jezebel. This woman persuaded her husband to do wicked things. First he murdered his six brothers; then he worshiped idols; and finally he made the people of his land worship false gods.

To punish Jehoram, God let the Philistines and the Arabians come into his cities and carry away all his treasures. They killed all the king's sons except the youngest. God sent Jehoram a terrible sickness from which he died.

Then, Ahaziah became king. He was bad like his father, for his mother Athaliah persuaded him to act wickedly. Soon after he became king he went down to see his uncle, King Joram of Israel. The two kings decided to make war on Ramoth-gilead, a city which the Syrians had taken away from the Israelites. You remember that Ahab was killed when he tried to recapture this city.

Although in this second battle the Israelites were successful in taking the city, King Joram was wounded. He and Ahaziah went back to the city of Jezreel, leaving the army at Ramoth-gilead.

Both these kings were of the family of Ahab. God had punished Ahab for his wickedness. God had said that every man of Ahab's family would die a bloody death. Those who died in the city would be eaten by the dogs, and those who died in the country would be eaten by the birds. God had said also that Jezebel would meet a violent death, and that dogs would eat her body by the wall of Jezreel.

Part of this prophecy had already been fulfilled in the death of Ahab. God was going to send a rough and violent man to carry out the rest of the punishment upon Ahab's family and upon Jezebel.

This man was Jehu, one of the captains of the army of Joram, king of Israel. Jehu was a very energetic, forceful sort of man, quick to action. Whatever he did was done with force and decision.

The prophet Elisha was still living in Israel. One day he summoned one of the young prophets, gave him a jar of oil, and told him to go to Ramoth-gilead, where the Israelite army was camped.

The young prophet took the oil and went to Ramoth-gilead. There he found Jehu sitting with the other captains of the army. The messenger from Elisha said, "I have an errand to you, O captain."

"To which one of us?" Jehu asked.

"To you, captain," replied the young prophet.

Jehu stood up and went into the house with the young man. The prophet poured the oil on Jehu's head, saying at the same time, "Thus says the Lord God of Israel, 'I have anointed you king over the people of the Lord, even over Israel. You shall destroy the family of your master, because he has killed My servants and prophets. Jezebel also has killed them. Therefore the whole house of Ahab shall perish. The dogs shall eat Jezebel in Jezreel, and no one shall bury her.'"

When the prophet had said this, he opened the door and ran away as fast as he could. Jehu went outside again to the place where all the officers were sitting. They asked, "What did this crazy fellow say to you?"

At first Jehu would not tell them. "Oh, you know what kind of man he is," he said.

But the officers were not satisfied with this answer. "That is not the truth," they cried. "Tell us truly what he said to you."

Finally Jehu decided to tell. "This is what he said to me: 'Thus saith the Lord, "I have anointed you to be king over Israel." ' "

The officers were glad. They hated the wicked family of Ahab, who had killed the prophets of the Lord and forced the whole nation to become idol-worshippers. They had often wished that the Lord would punish him and take the kingdom away from his family.

Each of the officers took off his cloak and put it upon the stairs to make a carpet for Jehu to stand upon. They blew upon their trumpets loudly and shouted, "Jehu is king!"

All this took place in Ramoth-gilead. The whole army was still camped there, although King Joram and King Ahaziah had gone back to the city of Jezreel after the battle. Being a man of action, Jehu commanded that the gates of the camp be shut, so that no one might go to Jezreel to tell Joram that Jehu had been made king.

All the captains got into their chariots and drove furiously to Jezreel, where many members of Ahab's family were staying. King Joram, who was Ahab's son, was there. So too was Ahaziah, king of Judah. He was Ahab's grandson, for his mother Athaliah was Ahab's daughter. The end of all Ahab's family was very near.

PART 2 — THE END OF AHAB'S FAMILY

There was a tower in Jezreel where a watch was kept night and day lest an enemy might approach. As the watchman was gazing this way and that over the country, he spied a cloud of dust in the distance. Soon he saw that it was a company of horsemen. He sent word to the king.

King Joram sent a man on horseback to meet the men who were approaching and ask if they came in peace. The messenger galloped out of the gates. When he came to Jehu he asked, "Is it peace?"

"What have you to do with peace?" said Jehu. "Stay here behind me. Do not return to the king."

The watchman on the tower sent word to King Joram that he had seen the man gallop away and speak to the horsemen, but that the messenger did not come back.

The king sent a second man with the same message. Jehu answered again, "What have you to do with peace? Stay here with me."

The watchman on the tower sent word again to the king, saying, "The second man went, but he does not come back. I think it must be Jehu who is coming, for he drives furiously."

Since Jehu was the leader of the army, Joram thought that he might be coming to tell him that the Syrians or some other enemy were making war on some of the cities. He sent for his chariot and for the chariot of King Ahaziah. Together the two kings drove out to meet Jehu. As soon as he was near enough, Joram called out anxiously, "Is it peace, Jehu?"

But Jehu shouted back, "How can there be any peace, as long as your wicked mother has done all this evil?"

King Joram saw at once that something was wrong. He turned his chariot around to escape. As he went, he called out to King Ahaziah, "There is treachery, O Ahaziah!"

Jehu was a very quick and strong man. In an instant, he drew his bow with his full strength and shot King Joram through his heart. The king sank down dead in his chariot.

Jehu said to his captains, "Throw his body into the field of Naboth. When Ahab was king, the Lord said to him, 'I will punish you in Naboth's field.'"

When King Ahaziah saw what happened to King Joram, he turned his chariot and fled. Jehu hastened after him, calling to his captains,

"Shoot him, too!" The captains killed Ahaziah, for he was of the family of Ahab. His servants carried their dead king back to the kingdom of Judah and buried him with the kings in the city of David.

Jehu and his company drove on till they reached the city of Jezreel, where Jezebel lived. When the Queen heard what Jehu had done, she painted her face and combed her hair. She leaned out of an upstairs window.

As Jehu entered the palace gate, Jezebel called to him. He did not listen to her. He shouted, "Who is on my side?" Two or three men-servants looked out at him. He called to them, "Throw her down!"

The servants pitched Jezebel out of the window headfirst. She struck on the stones below and was killed. Her blood spattered on the wall and on Jehu's horses. He drove his chariot over her body, trampling her under the feet of his horses.

After he had eaten his dinner he said to some of his servants, "Look after that wicked woman and bury her, for she is a king's daughter." But when the soldiers went to bury the queen, the wild dogs of Jezreel had eaten her.

Jehu's work was not yet done. Ahab had had many wives and many sons. There were seventy of his sons living in Samaria who must be killed. Jehu wrote letters to the men who were in charge of Ahab's sons, commanding them to kill these seventy sons; for all the family of Ahab had to be destroyed. As long as any of Ahab's sons were left, the country could not get away from idolatry.

On the road Jehu met a company of forty-two young men, the nephews of King Ahaziah, who were going to visit their cousins. Jehu's soldiers killed them too, for they were the grandchildren of King Ahab.

Jehu did not spare a single man of Ahab's family. Wherever he found any of Ahab's relatives he killed them, so as to obey God's command to rid the land of that wicked family. He did not kill all the women, for God had not commanded him to destroy them. As you will soon see; it would have been a good thing if he had gone into Judah and killed Athaliah, the wicked daughter of Ahab and Jezebel.

PART 3 — BAAL IS DEAD!

After Jehu had killed all Ahab's family, he had another important task. He had to drive idolatry out of the land.

In Samaria, almost all the people were idolaters, for King Ahab and Queen Jezebel had made them worship idols. Jehu wanted to gather all the prophets and priests of Baal together, so that he could kill every one of them, and thus wipe idolatry out of the Lord's country.

In order to get hold of every one of these prophets, Jehu played a trick. He announced to the people of Samaria that he would serve Baal much more than Ahab had ever done. He would make a great sacrifice, to which all the priests and worshippers of Baal must come. If any worshipper of Baal should not come to the sacrifice, he would be killed.

From all over the country, the worshippers of Baal came to the sacrifice. They were afraid to disobey a man so harsh as Jehu had shown himself to be.

Jehu met a man named Jehonadab, a true worshiper of God. He said, "Come with me and see how hard I am working for God." He took Jehonadab up into his chariot with him. Together they went to the temple of Baal.

The temple was filled from one end to the other with the worshippers. They stood crowded together, barely able to breathe. Jehu and Jehonadab tried to crowd into the doorway of the temple, but they could not get in. Jehu shouted to the people, "See that there are none of the worshippers of the Lord here, but only the worshippers of Baal."

Jehu and Jehonadab went outside. Jehu said to the man who kept the robes which the worshippers of Baal wore in the temple, "Get robes for all the men inside the temple."

Then he took eighty men and placed them all around the outside of the temple. He said to them, "If you let any of those men escape, you yourselves will be killed to pay for it." Turning to his soldiers, he said, "Go into the temple of Baal and kill all those men. Do not let one of them escape."

The soldiers obeyed Jehu. Not one of the worshippers of Baal escaped. The guard outside recognized them by their robes, and killed those who evaded the soldiers.

Jehu sent his soldiers into the temple to bring out all the images that were there, and burn them. The image of Baal was broken down. Of the temple itself Jehu's soldiers made a rubbish heap.

Ahab and all his family had died as the prophet foretold. Jehu had destroyed the priests and prophets of Baal and all his worshippers. The images had been burned and the temple of Baal had been pulled down. All these things were necessary, for the wicked family of Ahab had turned the people away from the true God to the worship of Baal. God had been almost forgotten in the land.

God had sent this rough-and-ready Jehu to rid the land of Ahab's family and of the worship of Baal. A gentler man than Jehu could not have done it. Jehu was rewarded for his work. God told him that he would be king, and his sons would be kings after him for four generations.

Now the people of Israel might have turned back to the Lord, if they had had anyone to teach them the ways of God. But Jehu, although he was a great soldier, was no teacher. He destroyed the worship of Baal, but he did not try to teach the people to worship God. The people of Israel had become so idolatrous that they could not understand how they could worship a God whom they could not see.

When the first king of Israel, Jeroboam, had divided the kingdom of Israel from the kingdom of Judah, he had set up two golden calves, so that the children of Israel would not have to go to Jerusalem to worship. These golden calves were still worshipped. This was not like the service of the heathen idol Baal, for the two calves were supposed to represent the true God.

Of course it was not right for the people to worship these golden calves. In the Ten Commandments God had told the Israelites not to bow down to any image. But the people of the kingdom of Israel had been worshipping idols so long that they thought they could not worship a God whom they could not see. And so in spite of all the good that Jehu had done, he did not take away the golden calves, and the people kept on worshipping them.

How foolish and wrong it seems to us now! We know that we can worship God and pray to Him, even if we cannot see Him.

Even in Israel, not all the people worshipped the calves. God sent many prophets to teach the people about the Lord. Some of the people listened to the prophets and worshipped their own God in the right way.

God was going to send a severe punishment to the Israelites for forgetting Him. After many years He would let them be conquered by the powerful kings beyond the Euphrates River. They would be carried away from their own land to countries far away.

In Jehu's reign God began this punishment. He let Hazael, the king of Syria, come to fight against the Israelites on the east side of the Jordan. Hazael destroyed many of the towns of the tribes of Gad, Manasseh, and Reuben.

King Hazael was very cruel in his victories. Elisha had wept when he saw how Hazael would burn the cities of the Israelites, and kill their young men with the sword, and dash their babies to death on the stones. All this came to pass in the reign of Jehu.

CHAPTER 88

The Little Boy Who Became King

II Kings 11, 12; II Chronicles 22, 23, 24

| King of Israel | King of Judah |
| Jehu | Joash |

Part 1 — How Joash Was Kept Safe

While Jehu was king in Israel, what was happening in the kingdom of Judah?

Jehu killed King Ahaziah because he was the grandson of Ahab. Ahaziah had reigned only one year. Even in that short time he did evil in the sight of the Lord, for his wicked mother Athaliah persuaded him to do as Ahab had done.

After Ahaziah was dead, Athaliah became a monster of wickedness. She killed Ahaziah's children, her own grandchildren! She did not want them to be kings; she wanted to reign.

But one little baby was saved. When Ahaziah's sister saw that the grandmother was killing all the little princes, she stole the littlest one, a tiny baby, and hid him with his nurse in a bedroom. She kept him close by her, and never let his grandmother see him. His name was Joash. For six years his aunt kept the little boy hidden away from his blood-thirsty grandmother, who had made herself queen.

The aunt was married to a very good man named Jehoiada, who was the high priest of God. Little Joash was hidden in the Temple of the Lord. He was safe there, for Athaliah never went near the Temple.

No one knew that one of the sons of King Ahaziah was still alive. His aunt and uncle kept the secret.

When little prince Joash was seven years old, the priest Jehoiada sent for all the captains of the army to come to Jerusalem. He told them that when wicked Queen Athaliah had killed the princes, one little baby had been saved. He made them swear to be true to the little Joash.

The captains were glad to make this promise, for they hated Queen Athaliah, because she was very wicked. Besides, she was a foreigner, not of the royal line of David. They wanted a king of David's line.

Things had seemed very dark to the people of Judah. The wicked Athaliah had caused her husband Jehoram to kill all his brothers, the six other sons of Jehoshaphat. She had killed all her grandchildren, so far as the people knew. The people could not understand why God should let the whole royal line of David be wiped out. God had promised David that his children should rule forever; but how could this be, when all the family of David had been killed?

You can imagine with what joy the people heard that one prince of the royal line had been saved. Jehoiada brought out the little Joash and showed him to the captains of the army. He commanded all the soldiers to stand close around the little prince to keep him from harm.

After he had placed this armed guard around the prince, he invited all the people of Judah to come to the crowning of their king. He put the crown upon the little boy's head, anointing him with oil. Joash was king! The sound of trumpets burst forth, and the people clapped their hands, shouting, "Long live the king! Long live the king!"

Queen Athaliah heard the noise of the shouting and the blare of the trumpets. She came to the Temple to see what the uproar was about. There she saw the little king standing by a pillar in the Temple, and all the soldiers around him with spears and shields. The people were clapping their hands and rejoicing.

The queen tore her clothes and threw up her hands, screaming, "Treason! Treason!"

Jehoiada commanded the soldiers to kill her, but not in the holy Temple. Athaliah ran out into the driveway of the horses. There the soldiers killed the wicked woman who had caused so many deaths.

Jehoiada made all the people promise that they would be the Lord's people. The little king had to promise that he too would serve the Lord.

Then the people went into the temple of Baal and broke it down. The grandchildren of Ahab had brought in the worship of Baal, even to the holy city of Jerusalem.

Forming a great procession, the people brought the little king into the king's royal palace. They lifted him up to the king's throne. There he sat, with the king's golden crown on his head and the king's golden scepter in his hand. How small he must have looked on that grand throne!

Joash was only seven years old when he was made king. He served the Lord, for the good priest Jehoiada had brought him up and taught him about God.

Not long before, the whole nation of Judah had been God-fearing. Joash's grandfather Jehoshaphat had been a good king, and had reigned twenty-five years. His son Jehoram had married the bad Athaliah and had worshiped idols. He had reigned only eight years, and his son Ahaziah had been on the throne only one year. Even though wicked Queen Athaliah had seized the throne for six years, only fifteen years had passed since the days of good King Jehoshaphat.

Most of the people could remember those days. They were very happy when they saw that little Joash was growing up to be a good and God-fearing man. God let King Joash reign for forty years.

PART 2 — JOASH FORGETS GOD

When the boy Joash grew up, it came into his heart to repair God's holy Temple. Almost one hundred fifty years had passed since Solomon built the Temple. Some parts had become worn out and needed to be repaired. The sons of Athaliah had taken out many of the golden dishes and put them into the temple of Baal.

King Joash told the old priest Jehoiada to take the money that the people brought, and to use it to pay workmen. Some of the carpenters made a strong chest. In the top of it they bored a hole big enough for the money to go through. They set the chest beside the gate of the Temple.

When any man came to the Temple to give an offering to the Lord, he dropped the money into the box. Moses, long ago, had commanded that every man twenty years old should bring half a shekel to the Lord every year. Joash ordered the people of the land to bring that offering to the Temple.

The people were so pleased to have their beautiful Temple built up again that they brought a great deal of money into the chest. When the chest was filled, the high priest and the king's scribe took out the money and put it into bags. Every day the chest became full, and was emptied.

The money was used to pay the men who worked on the Temple, and to buy timber and hewed stone to repair the walls of the building. The money that was left was used to buy golden and silver dishes for the service of the Lord. At last the Temple was finished. Once again it was stately and splendid.

As long as the good old priest Jehoiada lived, King Joash was a good ruler. But Jehoiada was already ninety years old when Joash was crowned. At last the priest died, at the age of one hundred thirty years. The people loved him so much for all the good he had done that they buried him with the kings in the city of David.

After Jehoiada's death, some very sad things happened. I wish I could leave them out, but nothing can be left out of a Bible story.

The princes of Judah came to King Joash and said that they were tired of worshipping the Lord. They wanted to return to their idol worship. Since Joash himself felt the same way, the people left the Lord, and returned to the idols, Baal and the Asherim.

God sent some prophets to them to make them turn back to Him, but they would not listen. The Spirit of God came upon Zechariah, the son of the good old priest Jehoiada, telling him to say to the people that they would not prosper if they should continue to forget God.

But the king and the people would not listen to Zechariah. Joash told the people to pick up big stones and throw them at the son of the good old priest who had saved the little prince from his blood-thirsty grandmother Athaliah, and who had crowned him king! What made it still worse was that this happened in the court of the holy Temple.

Just before Zechariah died, he said, "May the Lord remember what they have done, and punish them for it."

God did punish Joash and his people for their sins.

I am sure you remember Hazael, the king of Syria, who murdered Ben-hadad by smothering him with a wet cloth held tight over his face. God used this merciless man to punish the kingdom of Israel and the kingdom of Judah for their idol-worship.

Hazael came against Israel, which was nearer to Syria than Judah. Although the son of Jehu, who was now on the throne, had not followed the Lord, he prayed to God when danger threatened him. God heard him and turned away the army of the Syrians.

Then King Hazael marched on to Judah and Jerusalem. He did not have a large army, but God allowed him to kill all the princes of Judah, because they had forgotten the God of their fathers. Seeing this, Joash took all the sacred things and all the gold out of the Temple and sent them to Hazael, to bribe him to go away from Jerusalem.

Many of the people of Judah became very angry with their king. He had begun his reign so well by repairing the Temple of the Lord, but ended it so badly by forsaking the God of his fathers.

Two of the servants of Joash thought that he deserved to die, because he had murdered Zechariah, the son of the good old priest who had brought him up. One night, they made up their minds that they were going to kill the king. They slipped into the bedroom where he lay sick, and they killed him.

When the people of Judah found that their king was dead, they buried him, but not in the graves of the kings. They did not think he deserved that honor, for he had turned away from the Lord.

King Joash had begun to reign when he was seven years old. He ruled for forty years. If he had obeyed God, he might have reigned for many years longer.

CHAPTER 89

Elisha's Last Prophecy

II KINGS 13

Kings of Israel	*Kings of Judah*
Jehu	Joash
Jehoahaz	Amaziah
Jehoash	

Although Joash was only forty-seven years old when he was murdered, he had reigned forty years. During these years, three kings reigned in Israel. They were all of Jehu's line, for God had promised Jehu that, because he destroyed the whole wicked family of Ahab, his sons should be kings of Israel for four generations.

Jehu had been king for seven years before Joash was crowned king of Judah. He reigned in Israel for twenty-one years longer, before he died. Although he had destroyed the idols of Baal and all the priests of Baal, he did not destroy the golden calves that were in Bethel and in Dan. The people still worshipped these calves as God.

Jehu's son Jehoahaz became king after him. He also worshipped the golden calves, exactly as God had told the Israelites not to do, in the Ten Commandments. God punished the Israelites for bowing down to the golden calves, by letting Hazael, the cruel king of the Syrians, come to fight against them. He listened to their prayers; when they turned to Him, He caused the Syrians to go back to their own country, although Hazael left Jehoahaz only fifty horsemen and ten chariots and ten thousand soldiers.

Jehoahaz reigned only seventeen years. Then he died and his son Jehoash became king. He worshipped the golden calves, as his father had; yet he was not as bad as King Ahab had been.

In the days of Jehoash the kind old prophet Elisha, who had lived in the kingdom of Israel all these years, became very sick. The king was sad when he heard that he was soon going to lose his friend, the prophet. Elisha had helped him to govern his kingdom. He had given him good advice. Who would help the king to govern and fight when Elisha was gone? Who would pray to the Lord for him?

With these sad thoughts Jehoash went to see Elisha, who lay on his bed, pale and weak. Big tears rolled down the king's cheeks, as he sobbed, "My father, my father!"

Elisha, sick and weak, said to the king in a feeble voice, "Take bow and arrows."

The king went into the next room, and found a bow and arrows. He came back to Elisha's bedside with them. The prophet said weakly, "Put your hand upon the bow."

The king stretched the bow in his strong young arms. With a great effort, the sick prophet raised himself to a sitting position, leaned over and laid his thin white hands over the king's strong brown ones. "Open the window," he said. When the window was open, he said, "Shoot!"

As the king shot an arrow, Elisha said, "The Lord's arrow of victory, even the arrow of victory over Syria; for you shall smite the Syrians till you have conquered them."

Then he said, "Take the arrows and strike the ground." The king struck the ground three times with the arrows. Elisha said, "Why didn't you strike the ground five or six times? Then God would have helped you to conquer the Syrians utterly. Now, He will give you the victory only three times."

The old prophet fell back upon the bed, exhausted. Soon afterwards he died and was buried.

Not long after Elisha's death, another man died. While his friends were burying him, they saw a band of robbers approaching. In their fear and their hurry to get away, they dropped the body of their friend into the first grave they saw. This happened to be Elisha's. As soon as the body of the dead man touched the bones of Elisha, he revived and stood up on his feet.

Elisha's prophecy about Jehoash's victory over the Syrians came true. Hazael, that cruel Syrian king who had murdered his master, died. His son, who was also named Ben-hadad, became king. It seems strange that Hazael should give his son the name of the king whom he murdered.

Jehoash went to fight with this second Ben-hadad three times. Just as Elisha had said, Jehoash conquered the second Ben-hadad three times. He got back the Israelite cities which Hazael had taken away from Israel.

CHAPTER 90

A Proud King Defeated

II Kings 14; II Chronicles 27

King of Israel	*King of Judah*
Jehoash	Amaziah

While Jehu and Jehoahaz and Jehoash were reigning in Israel, the boy-king Joash ruled in Judah. As I have told you, he was murdered by his servants when he was forty-seven years old.

His son Amaziah was king of Judah at the time when Jehoash was king of Israel. Like his father Joash, he was a good king in the early years of his life; and, like his father, he did wrong later.

Amaziah tried to make a strong army to defend his kingdom. He numbered all the able-bodied men, able to go to war. There were three hundred thousand of them. For one hundred talents of silver Amaziah hired one hundred thousand brave men out of Israel. He thought that with such an army he could go to fight any of the heathen nations and conquer them.

A prophet of God came to him with a warning. "O king," he said, "do not let the army of Israel go with you, for God will not help the

Israelites in battle. He is angry with them for worshipping the golden calves."

Amaziah objected, "But I have already paid them a hundred talents of silver. If I let them go home, I shall lose all that money."

"Never mind about the money," the prophet replied. "God is able to give you much more money than that."

Amaziah obeyed the prophet and let the Israelite soldiers go home. One would think that those soldiers ought to have been satisfied. They got their pay without going to war. Strangely enough, they were angry to be sent home without doing any fighting. They went to some of the cities of Judah in revenge and killed three thousand people.

Even after these Israelites had gone home, Amaziah still had a big army of his own men. With his three hundred thousand men of Judah, he went to the Valley of Salt, south of the Dead Sea, where the Edomites lived. He fought against them and won the battle.

In Edom, King Amaziah saw some heathen idols. He brought them home with him and set them up in his house. We are apt to say that none of us today could be so foolish as to worship senseless images. Yet Amaziah was really no worse than many foolish people nowadays who like to go to a fortune teller and have their fortunes predicted, although no fortune teller really knows anything about the future.

God was angry with Amaziah for worshipping the idols of Edom. He sent a prophet to King Amaziah with the warning message, "Why have you worshipped the gods of Edom when you saw that those idols could not help even their own people?"

But Amaziah was so proud of his victory, that he wanted to win some more. He sent word to King Jehoash, king of Israel, saying that he wanted to fight with him.

King Jehoash had just come home from fighting with the Syrians. He had won some splendid victories over the Syrian king, winning back the cities that his father had lost. He did not want to fight and cause the death of his soldiers. He sent word to King Amaziah, "You are feeling very proud because you have conquered those few Edomites. It is very foolish for you to come to fight with me, for I have many more soldiers than you have. I warn you that you will be beaten, and many of your people will be killed."

Amaziah would not listen. God was going to let him be beaten in order to punish him for worshipping idols.

The armies met. King Amaziah suffered a dreadful defeat. Worse than that, King Jehoash marched on to Jerusalem and broke down a large part of the high stone wall of the city. Then he went to the Temple and took all the gold and silver that he could find. He marched to the king's palace and took away all the treasures.

Soon after this battle, Jehoash, king of Israel, died. His son Jeroboam became king. Amaziah lived fifteen years longer. They were not happy years, for his people were angry with him. They blamed him for the defeat which had spoiled their city and Temple, and brought about so many deaths.

The people of Judah began to wish they had no king to lead them into foolish and unnecessary wars, and turn them away from God to worship idols. They began to talk about punishing the king for what he had done.

A rumor of this talk came to the king's ears. He thought he had better run away before these plans could be put into action. He fled down to Lachish, in the country of the Philistines. Some of his soldiers chased after him. They killed him in Lachish and brought his body back to Jerusalem.

Amaziah, like his father Joash, began his reign in the fear of God, and ended it by turning away to worship idols. Like his father, too, he was killed by his own people. In spite of these sad experiences, the people made Uzziah, Amaziah's son, king. He was only sixteen years old.

CHAPTER 91

Jonah, the Unwilling Prophet

Jonah

| King of Israel | King of Judah |
| Jeroboam II | Uzziah |

Part 1 — Running Away From God

During the long reigns of Uzziah and Jeroboam II, we shall leave the two kingdoms for a while, and take a journey to the far-away city of Nineveh.

Nineveh was five hundred miles from Judah. It was the capital of Assyria, which, at that time, was the greatest country in the world. Nineveh was a very big city of three million people. It was very rich and splendid, full of wonderful palaces and temples. But since it was a heathen city, it was a very wicked one.

It happened that in the days of King Jeroboam II there was in Israel a prophet of the Lord, named Jonah. The Lord spoke to Jonah, and told him to go to the great city of Nineveh, to tell the people of the city that unless they turned away from their wickedness God would destroy their city.

But Jonah, although he was a prophet of the Lord, did not want to obey God. Instead of starting on the long journey to Nineveh, across the sandy desert, he walked off in exactly the opposite direction in order to run away from God.

He went down to Joppa on the sea-coast. At Joppa he found a ship that was going to Tarshish in Spain. He paid his fare and went into the ship. He was going to go far away to escape from God.

But Jonah could not run away from God! God is everywhere!

Uzziah had engines placed on the towers of Jerusalem. 2 Chronicles 26

"I have found a man who can tell the king his dream and its meaning."

Daniel 2

Down into the hold of the ship Jonah went. He lay down and fell fast asleep. The sailors loosened the ropes and hoisted the sails. The wind filled the sails, and the ship glided gracefully away from the harbor of Joppa and out into the open sea.

God saw Jonah disobeying Him. He sent a great wind over the sea. The blue sky became overcast with black clouds. The winds began to howl and roar. Great billows tossed the ship hither and thither. One moment the ship rose to a fearful height on the top of a mounting wave, and then it fell to a dizzy depth. Great waves swept over the deck.

The sailors were in terror of their lives. They cast out all the freight into the sea, to make the ship lighter. They called upon their gods to save them.

Jonah lay fast asleep in the hold. There the shipmaster found him, lying stupidly asleep and paying no attention to the danger they were in. The shipmaster shook him awake and said to him sharply, "What do you mean by sleeping at such a time as this? Wake up and pray to your God to save us."

"Someone must have done wrong and displeased his God," the sailors began to say to one another. "God is sending this storm to punish him. Let us cast lots, and find out who is the guilty one."

When the sailors cast lots, the lot fell on Jonah. The frightened men gathered around him and said, "Tell us what you have done to make your God angry and bring this fearful storm upon us."

Jonah said to them, "I am a Hebrew. My God is the God of Heaven. He made the sea and the dry land." The sailors were very much frightened when they heard this. Jonah told them how he was disobeying his God and running away, so that he would not have to go to Nineveh to preach to the people about their wickedness.

Jonah himself began to realize how wicked he had been. He knew that God was sending this storm to punish him for his disobedience.

"Why did you disobey your great God?" asked the sailors. "What shall we do to you, so that the sea may be calm for us?"

Jonah knew that God had sent the storm to punish him alone. He said to them, "Take me up and throw me into the sea. That will calm the waves. This great tempest has come to punish me only." The prophet thought that God was surely going to drown him, but if he were thrown into the sea, God would save the sailors. It was only he who deserved to die for disobeying God.

The sailors hated to do as Jonah said. They rowed with all their might, trying to bring the ship to the shore.

It was of no use. The storm became worse. The waves rose higher and higher, dashing into the ship and threatening to sweep the rowers into the sea. The sailors saw that they could do nothing in this angry storm. They realized that unless they did as Jonah said, they all would soon be drowned.

They were honest, upright people. They came together and cried unto the Lord, "We beseech Thee, O Lord, not to blame us for drowning this man; for it is Thou, Lord, who hast sent this storm."

Then they threw Jonah overboard into the wild, raging sea. At once the water became calm. The men knew that God had sent the storm as a punishment to Jonah. They believed in God. They offered a sacrifice to Him, and promised that they would worship Him all the rest of their lives.

But Jonah — what became of him? Down, down, down, sank Jonah! The waves and billows passed over him. The weeds tangled about his head. God caused a very large fish to come in Jonah's way. This huge fish opened its mouth and swallowed Jonah, just in time to save him from drowning. Here in the big fish Jonah was safe. There was air enough for him to breathe.

Jonah remained in the big fish for three days and three nights. He had time enough now, to think how nearly he had been drowned. He was so thankful to God for saving his life, that he made a beautiful prayer of thanksgiving while he was in the fish's belly.

After three days, the Lord spoke to the fish, so that it vomited Jonah upon the dry land.

PART 2 — A PROPHECY THAT DID NOT COME TRUE

Again the word of the Lord came to Jonah, telling him a second time to go to Nineveh and bring to it the warning that God told him to bring.

This time Jonah obeyed God at once. He started on the long, long journey. He must have traveled either on an ass, or on a camel. He had many miles to go over sandy deserts. It must have taken him many days to make the journey.

At last he reached the splendid city of Nineveh, in the far eastern land of Assyria. He began to walk through the streets of the city; and as he went, he cried in a loud voice,

"Yet forty days and Nineveh shall be overthrown! Yet forty days and Nineveh shall be overthrown!"

All the people stopped to listen to this strange message, asking, "Who is that man?" and "What does he say?"

Someone answered, "He says he is a prophet of the great God who made the world. His God has sent him here to say that in forty days our city shall be destroyed because of its wickedness."

When the people heard that this terrible punishment was coming upon the city, they were filled with fear. "What shall we do?" they cried. "What shall we do?"

They believed God. They proclaimed a fast. Everybody in the city refrained from eating. They laid away their fine silken garments and wore rough sackcloth — the rich people and the poor, the great and the humble.

The king of Nineveh also heard of Jonah's preaching. He arose from his throne, put off his splendid kingly robe, and covered himself with rough sackcloth. He sat in ashes instead of on his golden throne.

The king sent street criers throughout Nineveh, and had posters put up on all street corners with this message:

BY ORDER OF THE KING AND OF HIS NOBLES

Let neither man nor beast, herd nor flock, taste anything. Let them not feed nor drink water.

But let them be covered with sackcloth, both man and beast, and let them cry mightily unto God. Let them turn every one from his evil way, and from the violence that is in his hands.

Who can tell whether God will not turn and repent, and turn away His fierce anger, that we perish not?

When God saw that the people of Nineveh turned from their wickedness, He did not do the evil that He had said He would bring upon them. The city was not destroyed. Repentance and prayer saved it.

Jonah was very much displeased that God was merciful to the people of Nineveh, after the prophet had said that the city would surely be destroyed. He thought that now no one would ever believe him again. He wanted God to punish the city. He even dared to pray to God and to say:

"O Lord, that is just what I said when I was in my own country. That is the reason why I fled to Tarshish. I know that Thou art a gracious and merciful God, slow to anger and of great kindness. I was afraid that if I preached to the people of Nineveh, they would turn from their sins and would be forgiven. That is just what has happened. I would rather die than live, if Thou art going to forgive those people, after I have preached to them that their city is to be destroyed."

Jonah went out of the city and made himself a little arbor of branches of trees to shield him from the hot sun. He sat under it and watched to see if the Lord would listen to his prayer and destroy the city.

God made a fast-growing plant to come up out of the ground so as to make a nice shade over Jonah's arbor. Jonah was very glad of the shade of the big plant, for the sun was very hot.

The next day, the Lord sent a worm which ate the stem of the plant, so that it withered and no longer shaded Jonah's arbor. The sun beat down so hot upon his head that the prophet fainted and wished to die.

The Lord said to him, "You are sorry for the plant which came up in a night and withered in a night. Do you not think that I ought to pity that great city of Nineveh? Are there not sixty thousand people in that city who are not able to tell their right hand from their left?"

So God taught Jonah the lesson of mercy.

CHAPTER 92

Stories About the Two Kingdoms

II Kings 14, 15; II Chronicles 26, 27

Kings of Israel		*Kings of Judah*
Jeroboam II	Menahem	Uzziah
Zachariah	Pekahiah	Jotham
Shallum	Pekah	

Part 1 — Six Wicked Kings

Jeroboam II was king over Israel. He also had a long reign, for he ruled forty-one years. He was not a good man. He was the fourth king of Jehu's line. Like all the others of Jehu's family, he worshipped the golden calves.

Although Jeroboam was not a good king, he waged some very successful wars against the neighboring country of Syria, which had oppressed the Israelites for many years. The children of Israel suffered so much from the cruelty of the Syrians that God was sorry for them. He saved them through Jeroboam. God gave King Jeroboam great victories over the enemy. The Israelites recovered some of their cities from the Syrians. Israel became a large country again, as it had been in Solomon's time.

But for all that, King Jeroboam worshipped the golden calves. In his days the people of Israel lived lives of luxury and drunkenness. God was forgotten in the land. The rich people oppressed the poor.

God sent the prophets, Amos and Hosea, to bring the people back to God. The prophet Amos said to the people of Israel that God would punish them for their sins and their idolatry. Their king Jeroboam would be killed and they would be carried away into captivity.

One of the false prophets told Jeroboam what the prophet Amos was saying. The false prophet then told Amos that he must leave the land of Israel, and go down into Judah, where his prophecies might be more welcome.

Amos answered, "You say, 'Do not prophesy against Israel.' But God told me, 'Go prophesy to My people Israel. Israel shall surely go into captivity.' "

Centuries before the time of Amos, Moses had solemnly warned the children of Israel that if they forgot God and worshipped idols, He would take them away from the good land which He had given to them. They forgot this warning. For many long years they bowed down to idols. Now the Lord again sent them prophets to tell them that if they did not turn back to Him, He would surely send them away captive into a strange land.

Amos prophesied during the reign of Jeroboam II. That king was wicked, but the rulers who came after him were still worse.

At the death of Jeroboam, his son Zachariah became king. He reigned a very short time. He had been on the throne for only half a year, when Shallum, one of his servants, killed him. Thus the family of Jehu came to an end. As God had promised Jehu, his family had been kings of Israel for four generations.

Shallum, who had killed Zachariah, became king. He ruled for just one month, and then he was killed by a man named Menahem, who ruled for ten years. Menahem was a savagely cruel man. He made a raid into Syria and killed his captives with cruel torture.

This was the time when the great country of Assyria had become the strongest country in the world, very much larger than either Israel or Syria.

The king of Assyria came to fight against the little kingdom of Israel. If Menahem had been a good king, he would have prayed to the Lord to help him. But he gave no thought to God. He paid the king of Assyria a thousand talents of silver, so that he would not fight against Israel.

God was almost forgotten in Israel. The land was full of drunkenness and sin of every kind. The people worshipped the golden calves and other idols. They even gave their children to Moloch. They put a little child into the arms of this idol and then built a fire inside the image, until it was red-hot. The poor little child was burned to death. The people thought that the idol was pleased to have their little children sacrificed to him.

There was no goodness or peace in the land. The people had become utterly bad, like the heathen that were in the land before the Israelites.

After ten years, King Menahem died. His son, Pekahiah, became king. Pekahiah was no better than his father. He reigned only two years in Israel. Then one of his generals, named Pekah, killed him. Pekah reigned for twenty years.

During all this time, while Israel had six bad kings, there was only one ruler in the land of Judah. Good King Uzziah reigned there for many years.

PART 2 — A GOOD KING WHO BECAME A LEPER

Uzziah was only sixteen years old when he began to reign. He was king for fifty-two years in Jerusalem.

Uzziah did what was right, and the Lord made him prosperous. All the years when the kingdom of Israel was having such an unhappy time, killing their kings and worshipping idols, the kingdom of Judah was living in the fear of God, happy and prosperous.

King Uzziah went to fight against the Philistines. The Lord helped him to conquer the Philistine cities and to break down their walls. Uzziah subdued the Arabians, also. The Ammonites had to bring tribute to him.

He built strong fortified towers at the gates of Jerusalem. He repaired the city wall where it had been broken down. He had towers built in the desert, so that if any army should come up against him his soldiers in the towers might defend the country.

This wise king trained a big army of soldiers to help him to fight against their enemies. He had more than three hundred thousand soldiers, equipped with shields and spears and helmets. The army was provided with bows and slings to cast stones.

Uzziah had engines placed on the towers of Jerusalem, to be used for shooting arrows and big stones. These engines had been invented by the clever men of his kingdom. The people had never had anything like them before.

King Uzziah loved farming. He had vineyards and large flocks of sheep and cattle. He ordered a great many wells dug, so that his sheep and cattle might have enough water.

All these things were considered so wonderful in those days, that the fame of Uzziah spread far abroad, even to Egypt. He was marvelously helped by God. His kingdom became very strong.

But Uzziah's strength made him proud. He thought that he could go into the Temple to burn incense upon the golden Altar of Incense, just as the priests did.

Taking a censer, he went into the Temple. Some of the priests saw him go there with the censer. Eighty of the priests went after the king, saying, "You have no right to burn incense, Uzziah. That privilege belongs only to the priests of Aaron's tribe, who have been consecrated. God will be angry with you if you do this."

King Uzziah was annoyed with the priests for stopping him. While he was standing there, God punished him. The dreaded disease of leprosy appeared on his forehead. The priests looked in horror and astonishment at the deadly white spots on his forehead. At last they realized that King Uzziah had really been stricken with leprosy. They began to push him out of the Temple. As soon as Uzziah saw and felt he was a leper, he hurried away.

All the rest of his life, Uzziah had to live in a house alone. He could never go into the Temple again. Although he was still king, his son Jotham had to do the ruling.

At last, Uzziah died, after a very long reign of fifty-two years. He was buried with his fathers, and his son Jotham reigned.

For sixteen years Jotham was king in Jerusalem. Like his father, he did what was right in the sight of the Lord. Because Jotham worshipped the Lord, God helped him, and gave him success in his battles. Jotham became a mighty king.

He built castles and towers to make his kingdom strong, as Uzziah had done. Like Uzziah, too, he conquered his enemies. He fought against the Ammonites, and was victor over them.

The people were happy and prosperous when their kings feared the Lord.

After reigning sixteen years, King Jotham died. His son Ahaz became king.

CHAPTER 93

"Here Am I—Send Me"

Isaiah 6, 7, 9, 53

In these days there lived in the kingdom of Judah one of the greatest prophets the world has ever known. He was called Isaiah.

Isaiah was born in the last part of Uzziah's reign. He prophesied after Uzziah's death, during the reigns of the three succeeding kings. These prophecies were gathered together into a book. You may read them in the Bible.

In the year of King Uzziah's death, Isaiah had a wonderful vision. He saw God Almighty sitting upon a throne, high and lifted up, and surrounded by angelic beings called seraphim.

Each seraph had six wings. With two wings he covered his face, and with two he covered his feet, and with two he flew.

The seraphim cried aloud, "Holy, holy, holy is the Lord of hosts! The whole earth is full of His glory!" When the seraphim cried these words, the foundations of the Temple shook, and all the place was filled with smoke.

Isaiah was very much terrified to hear the voice of the mighty seraphim, and to feel the Temple shake, as it became filled with smoke. He feared he would die, because he, a sinner, had seen the Lord God.

Then one of the seraphim took a live coal from the altar, and flew with it to Isaiah. He placed it upon Isaiah's mouth, saying, "This has touched your lips, and your sin is taken away."

Isaiah heard the Lord say, "Whom shall I send, and who will go for us?"

"Here am I; send me," Isaiah answered.

The Lord gave Isaiah many messages to the children of Israel. The book of Isaiah is full of these wonderful prophecies. Isaiah foretold what was going to happen to Judah in the future.

The most wonderful of these prophecies are those which tell of the coming of Christ, which Isaiah wrote seven hundred years before Jesus was born.

As you remember, God promised Eve that through one of her children He would bring back goodness and everlasting life to man. God promised Abraham that in one of his descendants all the world would be blest. God gave promises to others, that some day a child would be born who would be the Savior of the world.

Some of the most glorious promises were given to Isaiah. Listen to some of the things he spoke about, hundreds of years before they came to pass:

> "A virgin shall conceive and bear a son,
> And shall call His name Immanuel."

This promise was repeated in other words.

> "Unto us a child is born, unto us a son is given.
> And the government shall be upon His shoulder.
> And His name shall be called
> Wonderful, Counsellor, Mighty God,
> Everlasting Father, Prince of Peace."

Isaiah prophesied Christ's suffering as well as His birth. He said:

> "He is despised and rejected of men,
> A man of sorrows, and acquainted with grief."

Isaiah knew that it was for our sins that Christ would suffer. He wrote:

> "He was wounded for our transgressions;
> He was bruised for our iniquities."

How well did the Israelites understand these prophecies? They knew that God would send them a Savior. These prophecies of Isaiah made them look forward all the more eagerly to the time when He would come. During all the seven hundred years before the birth of Christ, they waited and hoped for His appearance.

CHAPTER 94

The End of the Kingdom of Israel

II KINGS 16, 17; II CHRONICLES 28

Kings of Israel	King of Judah
Pekah	Ahaz
Hoshea	

PART 1 — HOW ISRAEL FOUGHT AGAINST JUDAH

Now I have a very sad story to tell. It is about the son of good Jotham — King Ahaz of Judah.

Although he was the son of good King Jotham, and the grandson of good King Uzziah, Ahaz was one of the very worst kings that Judah ever had. He undid all the good that his father and grandfather had done.

Ahaz made idols for Baal. He burned his children in the fire, as the wicked heathen did. He sacrificed to heathen gods on the hills and under every green tree.

When King Ahaz turned to idols, a great number of his people forsook the Lord, also. All the nations around them worshipped idols, and the people of Judah wanted to do whatever their neighbors did.

God sent an army against the men of Judah, to punish them for their sins. This army was made up of Syrians under their king, and Israelites under King Pekah. One of the worst things this wicked king Pekah ever did was to join with the king of Syria to fight against the people of Judah.

The king of the Syrians battled with King Ahaz ot Judah. God permitted the Syrians to conquer. They carried away great numbers of the people of Judah as captives to Damascus.

Pekah, the king of Israel, also had a great battle with Ahaz. In one day, Pekah's soldiers killed one hundred twenty thousand of the men of Judah. Besides, the Israelites carried away to Samaria two hundred thousand women and children of Judah to make slaves of them.

There was in Samaria a prophet of the Lord. He was horrified to think that the Israelites should bring back all those women and children of their own race as slaves.

The prophet went out to meet the soldiers as they returned from the war, and he said to them, "God delivered the men of Judah into your hands as a punishment for their sins. You have killed them. Now you intend to make slaves of the women and children. God is already very angry with you for your sins. You must give up those captives whom God is punishing."

Some of the chief men of the tribes of Israel came to the soldiers and said, "You shall not come into the city with your captives. We have already made the Lord angry. Do you want to offend Him still more?"

So the soldiers left the captives and all the treasures they had taken from Judah. The chief men of the tribes clothed all the captives with the garments which the soldiers had brought back. They gave them food and drink. The weak ones were put on asses, and all were permitted to go back to their own country.

But what a sad home coming that was! In thousands of homes the husband and father was dead. In thousands of homes the sons and daughters had been carried away to be slaves in Damascus.

This was indeed a severe punishment for idol-worship. But the lesson was not yet learned. Instead of praying to the Lord to save him from the Israelites and Syrians, King Ahaz sent to the great king of Assyria, begging him to come and help.

King Ahaz had to pay a great deal of money for this help. He took all the gold and silver out of the Temple and sent it to the king of Assyria. This king came as far as Damascus. He fought against that city, and killed its ruler.

Ahaz went up to Damascus to help in the battle. There he offered sacrifices before a heathen altar. He took a great fancy to that altar, and he sent a pattern of it back to the priest in Jerusalem. That bad priest made a copy of the heathen altar and set it up in Jerusalem, ready for use.

In Damascus, King Ahaz offered sacrifices to the heathen gods of Syria because he thought that they helped the Syrians. He believed that if he sacrificed to them, they might help him too. He never even thought of asking his own great God to help him.

When King Ahaz came back from Damascus, he worshipped the heathen gods of the Syrians on the altar which the priest had built. Worse than that, he closed the doors of the Temple of the Lord in Jerusalem. He also cut up the gold and silver dishes in the Temple. He had heathen altars built on every corner in Jerusalem, and in every city of Judah.

Ahaz made a great mistake in asking the king of Assyria to help him, for the kingdom of Assyria was trying to conquer the whole world at that time. Never before had it been able to conquer Damascus, which was the strongest city of Syria. As long as Damascus was not conquered, the kings of Assyria were kept from coming down to Israel, for Damascus was between Assyria and Israel.

Now that Damascus had fallen into the hands of the Assyrians, nothing stood in their way. Some of their kings would attack Israel next.

PART 2 — THE TEN LOST TRIBES

We have reached a chapter which is very sad indeed.

At last the dreadful punishment came upon the children of Israel. God could bear with them no longer. They were as sinful as the heathen who had been in the land before them, whom God had cast out.

Again and again the Lord sent prophets to say, "Turn from your evil ways and keep My commandments." But the people would not hear. Obstinately they refused to obey God, following the ways of the heathen.

They made images for worship. They bowed down before the two golden calves, and before the Asherah. They worshipped the sun and the moon and all the stars. They burned their sons and daughters in sacrifice to Moloch, and they used enchantments. Therefore the Lord was very angry with Israel.

After reigning twenty years, King Pekah was killed by Hoshea, who became king and ruled for nine years. He also did evil.

In the ninth year of Hoshea's reign, another great king of Assyria came against Israel. Since the city of Damascus had been conquered, there was nothing to prevent him from taking Samaria, the capital city of Israel. He made Hoshea his servant, and made him pay tribute.

After a little while, Hoshea rebelled. He did not send tribute, and he tried to get the king of Egypt to help him fight against Assyria.

When the great king of Assyria found out about this he marched to Samaria and besieged it for three years. Finally he overcame it and took its king prisoner. The people of Israel were made captive, and most of them were carried off to the land of Assyria. Because of their unfaithfulness, God would no longer let them live in their land as His people.

Oh, the weeping, the wailing, as the Israelites looked for the last time upon the dear homes that had come down to them from their grandfathers! How could they say good-bye to all they loved? How could they leave it, and never come back?

Far away into the distant land of Assyria the Israelites were driven. There they were scattered among the heathen nations. After many years they became mixed with the heathen nations. Nobody knows what became of them in the end. They are the ten "lost tribes" of the children of Israel.

These tribes were no longer God's people, because they had been disobedient. There is no further record about them in the Bible. They were lost and forgotten forever. The rest of our Bible story is about the people of Judah.

After the ten tribes had been taken away into Assyria, people from Babylon were brought to live in the land of Israel. Of course these were heathen nations. They did not know anything about God. They brought their own idols with them, and worshipped them. Because these people did not fear God, He sent lions among them, which killed some of them.

News of this happening was sent back to the king of Assyria. He commanded that one of the priests of the Israelites who had been taken captive must go back and teach the strangers how to worship the God of the land.

This command was carried out. One of the priests went back and taught the people how they should worship the Lord. This teaching did very little good, for these people had been brought up to idol-worship. They went on bowing down to the idols that they had brought with them from their own country, merely adding the worship of God to the worship of their own images.

Their children and grandchildren followed their example, and served both the Lord and idols. In after-years these people came to be known as "Samaritans." They were despised by the people of Judah, because they were not true Israelites.

CHAPTER 95

Hezekiah The Good

II KINGS 18, 19, 20 II CHRONICLES 29-32

PART 1 — A SERVANT OF GOD

How sad and pitiable was the condition of the children of Israel!

The ten tribes were far away from the land that had been promised to their fathers. They were captives in a strange land, with no hope of going back to their own country. Because of their sins, God had finally cast them off.

The condition of Judah was almost as sad. There were few people left in the land. Those few were very unhappy, for from almost every family someone had been killed in battle, or had been taken captive.

At least one good thing had happened. The wicked King Ahaz, who had led the people into sin, was dead. His son Hezekiah was king now. Although Hezekiah's father had been a bad man, his mother had been a good woman, the daughter of a prophet. She had brought up her son to fear the Lord.

Hezekiah was one of the best kings that ever ruled over Judah. From the beginning of his reign, he sought the Lord, as David had done, trying to undo the wicked deeds of his father. God was with Hezekiah, and prospered him in whatever he did.

During the reign of Ahaz, the Levites had been scattered abroad, because God's house was shut up, and there were no sacrifices. The Temple had become dirty and full of rubbish.

In the very first year of his reign, Hezekiah opened the doors of the Temple of the Lord which his father had closed. He gathered together all the Levites and priests, and told them to clean the temple. He knew that it was because their fathers had forgotten God that God had forsaken them.

The Levites went into the Temple to clean away all the dirt and filth there. They carried the rubbish out and threw it into the brook Kidron.

This work took eight days. When the Levites were finished, they went to King Hezekiah and said, "We have cleaned the whole Temple, and the Altar of Burnt Offering, and the Table of Show Bread, and all the dishes. We have replaced all the vessels that King Ahaz took away."

The service of God had been forgotten for so many years that it was very hard for anyone to know just how to worship God in the right way. This earnest young king did his very best to bring the people back again to the true worship.

He gathered the rulers of the city. Together they went up to the house of the Lord. There they offered a sin offering to atone for the great sin of Judah and Israel in turning away from God.

Hezekiah formed a choir of Levites, as King David had done so long ago. When the burnt offerings were made, the choir sang praises with the Psalms of David, and the priests sounded their trumpets. All the congregation worshipped with bowed heads.

The king invited any who wanted to bring thank-offerings to the Lord to come up and give. Many people responded generously.

The prophet Isaiah must have helped and advised Hezekiah in all this. He must have rejoiced to see the regular worship of God again established in Judah.

Now that King Hezekiah knew the people wanted to turn back to the Lord, he made up his mind to go still further, and to revive the feast of the Passover.

He sent letters inviting the people to come to Jerusalem to keep the Passover. These letters passed from city to city, not only through the country of Judah, but also through the countries which had once belonged to the kingdom of Israel.

When the king of Assyria conquered the land, he did not take all the Israelites into captivity. Some of the very poorest people had been left behind. Since these poor people had no king, Hezekiah asked them to join in the celebration of the feast.

In Judah all the people obeyed the message which the king sent out. Among the few Israelites who were left, however, most of the people had been worshipping idols for many years. They had forgotten all about the Passover.

"Come to the Passover? No, indeed! We are not going to Jerusalem for such foolishness as that!" they said mockingly.

Yet even from Israel some people obeyed the letter of Hezekiah, for in wicked Israel there always remained some families who still worshipped their own God.

A great number of people came to Jerusalem for the Passover. The people were so happy to have the Passover kept again that when the first seven days were up they decided to continue the happy time for another week. There was great joy in Jerusalem, for since the time of King Solomon there had not been such a feast.

King Hezekiah did another important thing. He caused the people to bring to the Temple a tenth of all their corn and wine and oil, and whatever else they raised. God had commanded that the priests and Levites were to attend to the service of God's holy Temple, and that they were not to have farms of their own.

For many years the priests had had a hard time. When the people neglected to bring gifts to the Lord, the priests had to go hungry.

Those times were over. Once again the people brought one-tenth of their corn and wine, their oil and honey, to the house of the Lord for His servants.

PART 2 — JERUSALEM IN DANGER

Since the people of Israel had been carried captive to Assyria the people of Judah lived in constant dread that the same thing might happen to them. They knew that they would never be strong enough to resist the Assyrian king, if he should come to their little kingdom and make war upon them.

After Hezekiah had been king for fourteen years, the very thing that they dreaded threatened to come upon them. King Sennacherib of Assyria came down into Judah with all his soldiers to take the people captive. Terror filled the hearts of the people of Judah as they heard of the coming of this mighty king.

But though Sennacherib was so great and had such a large army, King Hezekiah did not give up. He trusted in God to help him. He took counsel with all his princes. It was decided to stop up all the brooks that were outside the city, so that the armies of Sennacherib would have no drinking water.

Hezekiah did more than that. He built up the wall around Jerusalem, where it had been broken down. He made it much higher, and he placed a second wall outside the first one. How fast and how eagerly the people worked!

Hezekiah set captains over the soldiers. Gathering these leaders together, the good king spoke encouragingly to them. "Be strong and courageous," he said. "Do not be afraid of the king of Assyria, nor of all his soldiers. We have more to help us than they have. They have only human help, but we have the Lord our God to help us and to fight our battles."

It took great faith to trust in the Lord when the great king of Assyria came. Sennacherib was conquering all the world at that time, and was carrying off the people of the conquered countries to the land of Assyria. Onward he marched with his victorious armies, overcoming every nation in his way.

The Assyrians were cruel to the nations whom they conquered. Wherever their armies went, they left ruin. Towns became smoking heaps of ashes. Princes were tortured to death, and those who fought were killed without mercy. The main roads were choked with captives, and animals bearing plunder of all sorts which was being taken to Nineveh.

It was not strange that the men of Judah were in terror when they heard that this army was coming against them.

King Sennacherib did not come straight to Jerusalem. He first went to a city of the Philistines which he meant to conquer before going against the Jews. He sent some of his generals with a great host of soldiers to Jerusalem with a message to the Jews and to King Hezekiah.

These men came as near to the city of Jerusalem as they could, and called out. Some of the officers of the king's household came out to meet them. Then one of the generals said to them:

"Tell Hezekiah that the great king, the king of Assyria, says this: 'Why are you shutting yourselves up in Jerusalem? You all will die of hunger and thirst, for I will come and besiege your city. Is Hezekiah telling you that the Lord your God will deliver you out of the power of the king of Assyria? How can you expect your God to help you? This same Hezekiah has taken away all His altars, and has made you worship before only one altar.' "

Of course this man could not understand that the altars which had been destroyed were heathen. He went on to say, in the words of Sennacherib:

" 'Do you not know what I and my fathers have done to the people of other lands? If the gods of the other lands could not deliver their people from me, do you think that your God can? Do not let Hezekiah deceive you or persuade you to trust in your God. No god of any people was strong enough to deliver his people from me, and neither will your God be able to save you.' "

The Assyrian general shouted this message in the Jewish language, so that the common people standing on the wall of the city could understand it.

The officers of Hezekiah said, "Do not speak in the Jewish language, for all the common people to hear. Speak to us officers in the Syrian language, for we understand it."

But the general said bluntly, "No, indeed! We shall speak to the people on the wall in their own language, for our master told us to speak to the common people, and not to the officers." Coming even nearer, he shouted the message once more, at the top of his voice.

The people on the wall of Jerusalem heard the Assyrian general shout these words. They trembled with fear, but they did not say a word, for King Hezekiah had commanded them not to answer.

PART 3 — THE ANGEL OF DEATH

The Assyrian general brought a letter to King Hezekiah which repeated the boast he had shouted to the people on the wall—that no god had ever been able to save his people from King Sennacherib, nor ever would be able.

When King Hezekiah received this letter, he went up to the house of the Lord. He spread the letter out and prayed to God. He knew that the Assyrians had been able to destroy the gods of the heathen nations only because those gods were only idols and helpless. He prayed that the Lord would save the people from Sennacherib, so that all the kingdoms of the earth might know that He only is Lord.

After Hezekiah had prayed, he sent some men to the prophet Isaiah with this message:

"This is a day of trouble for us. It may be that the Lord will hear the words of Sennacherib, king of Assyria, which he wrote to insult the living God, and perhaps the Lord will punish him for speaking like this. Therefore, O Isaiah, pray to your God that He may help us."

Hezekiah's messengers told the prophet all the things that had been shouted out to the people on the wall, and all that had been written in the letter.

Isaiah gave an answer for the men to take back to Hezekiah. God had heard the prayer of Hezekiah against Sennacherib. Hezekiah need not be afraid of the boast which the king of Assyria had made. God would make Sennacherib return to his own land, where he would be killed.

It was not by his own power that the Assyrian king had been able to win all his battles. God gave him power to conquer, but now the Lord would show that Sennacherib had no power of his own.

Isaiah said to the messengers, "Tell Hezekiah that the king of Assyria shall not come into this city nor shoot an arrow against it, but he shall go home by the same way he came. God will defend this city, for His own sake and for His servant David's sake."

This message, coming straight from God, must have been a wonderful comfort to Hezekiah. He had trusted in the Lord, and God was going to answer his trust by taking care of the city.

That night, the angel of the Lord went out and struck down a hundred eighty-five thousand soldiers in the camp of the Assyrians. In the morning, they were found lying dead on the ground in the camp. The splendid Assyrian army was shattered.

Where was Sennacherib's power now? Gone, all gone, in a single night!

Shamed and humbled, the proud king turned his face homeward— a weak and powerless man, a king without an army. Some time afterward, as he went into the house of his god, his own sons took swords and stabbed him to death.

Do you think that the nations around Judah heard of this miraculous way in which God saved His people from the great king of Assyria? Of course they did. Many of them brought presents to the Temple of that wonderful God in Jerusalem, and to King Hezekiah.

Soon after this, King Hezekiah became very sick. The prophet Isaiah came to him and said, "Get ready to die, for your time has come."

When Hezekiah heard this, he felt very sad. Must he die so soon, while he was still young? He was only forty years old. He had hoped to have a long and prosperous reign!

Hezekiah turned his face to the wall. He began to weep. Bitter tears rolled down his cheeks.

He prayed to the Lord to let him live. "Remember, O Lord, how I have tried to please Thee, and how I have lived a good life, and have done that which is right."

The Lord answered Hezekiah's prayer before Isaiah had gone out of the city. He told the prophet to turn again and tell Hezekiah, "Thus says the Lord, 'I have heard your prayer, I have seen your tears, and I will heal you. In three days you will be well enough to go up to My holy Temple. I shall add fifteen years to your life.'"

I think that, of all men who have ever lived, Hezekiah was the only one who knew exactly when he would die. He lived just fifteen years longer. They were very happy years, for God was pleased with him, his people loved him, and the heathen honored him.

He enjoyed great riches and honor. He made himself treasuries for silver and gold, and for precious stones and all kinds of jewels. He made storehouses for corn and wine and oil, and barns for all his animals.

At last the promised fifteen years were over. Hezekiah slept with his fathers. He was buried in the finest of the tombs of the sons of David. All Judah and Jerusalem honored this good king.

CHAPTER 96

A Wicked King Who Repented

II KINGS 21; II CHRONICLES 33

After Hezekiah's death, his son Manasseh reigned in his stead. Manasseh ruled longer than any other king of either Israel or Judah. He was twelve years old when he became king, and he reigned fifty-five years.

You will expect me to say that he was a good king, like his father Hezekiah. How I wish I could say that! But Manasseh was probably the very worst king that Judah ever had. He was more like Ahab, the wicked king of Israel, than like his godly father Hezekiah.

He undid all the good that his father had done. He built up again all the idol altars that his father had broken down. He made altars for Baal, and caused Asherah to be worshipped. He bowed to the sun and the moon and the stars, building altars for them in the very courts of God's holy Temple.

Though it is hard to believe, he burned his own children in the arms of the dreadful heathen idol Moloch! This savage man shed very much innocent blood in Jerusalem.

He persuaded the people of Judah to be even more wicked than the nations whom God had destroyed before them.

The Lord sent prophets to Manasseh and to the people of Judah to warn them of their sin, but the people would not listen.

How could it be that the same people who so earnestly sought the Lord in Hezekiah's time should so soon turn to idolatry when Manasseh was king?

These were not the same people. The older generation had died with Hezekiah, and these were their children. The whole nation conformed to idol-worship. When they had a good God-fearing king, they turned back to God for a little while, but at bottom the nation was still a nation of idol-worshippers. Just as soon as their good king died, they or their children turned away from God.

Though God is very loving and merciful, He is also just. He cannot let wickedness go unpunished.

God determined to cause the people of Judah to be taken away into the far kingdoms of the earth, because of the things Manasseh did in Jerusalem. He would deliver them into the hands of their enemies, because they had done evil since the day their fathers had come out of Egypt.

God brought the captains of the Assyrian army against Judah. They took Manasseh and bound him with chains and carried him away captive to Babylon.

During his imprisonment in Babylon, Manasseh became a changed man. He remembered the God of his father. He began to pray very earnestly to God. The Lord heard his prayer and mercifully brought him back to Jerusalem to be king again.

Manasseh had learned that the Lord is the only God. He was a truly changed man. The rest of his life he tried to undo the wickedness that he had done before. He took away the idols that he had put into God's Temple. He sacrificed peace offerings and thank offerings to God. He commanded the people of Judah to serve the Lord. He was the only king who began his reign in wickedness, and ended it in goodness.

Manasseh's son Amon reigned only two years. In that short time, he did much evil. He sacrificed to all the images which his father had made, and which he did not have time to destroy before he died. Amon did not become good, as his father had, but he became worse and worse. After two years, his servants killed him in his own house.

The people of Judah, angry with the servants who had killed their king, put the murderers to death. They took Amon's little son, Josiah, who was only eight years old, and made him king.

CHAPTER 97

Stories About King Josiah

II KINGS 22, 23; II CHRONICLES 34, 35

PART 1 — GOD'S BOOK IS FOUND

Eight-year old Josiah was a little boy king, as Joash had been.

Unlike little Joash, Josiah did not have to be kept hidden and guarded. Nobody wanted to kill little King Josiah. Everyone wanted him to be the king. He was of David's line, the direct heir to the throne. The whole nation of Judah crowned Josiah king. They all watched over the safety of their little boy king.

Although Josiah was a young child, he proved that a child can serve the Lord. He did what was right, even at the very beginning of his reign. When Josiah was sixteen years old, he began to pray and to seek after God. A few years later, he began to clean out of Jerusalem all the idols and the altars of heathen gods.

Josiah stood and watched the men, directing them as they worked. He had them break down the metal and carved images of Baal, and grind them into little pieces, scattering the dust on the graves of those who had worshipped them.

Josiah even went through all the cities of Israel to destroy their idols. There had been no king in Israel since the people had been carried away. Josiah knew, moreover, that he was the rightful king of Israel as well as of Judah, because he was the direct descendant of David.

When Josiah visited the cities of Israel, he took workmen with heavy axes and hammers. Wherever they found any idols or heathen altars, the men smashed them into powder.

After all the idols had been destroyed, Josiah sent some skilled men to repair the Temple. It needed much repairing, for it had been neglected for many years.

When the men were busy in the Temple, Hilkiah, the high priest, found an old book hidden away in a corner. He was very much interested in it. He showed it to the scribe. When they came to read the book, they found it to be the book of the law of Moses.

The two men carried this book to the king. The scribe read to Josiah the words which Moses had written long ago.

If this was not the very same book which Moses had written, it was an exact copy. Eight hundred years had passed since Moses had written his book and put it into the Holy of Holies, beside the Ark of the Covenant. That first book may have become worn out, for Moses had told the priests that they should take the book out of the Holy of Holies once every seven years, and read it to the people.

The law had not been studied as it should have been. If it had been, the people would not have become wicked and idolatrous.

On the other hand, the law of the Lord had not been utterly forgotten. Good King Jehoshaphat had sent teachers throughout his kingdom to teach the people the law of the Lord. Each of these teachers had carried with him a copy of the book of the law, which some wise scribe had copied from the original book in the Holy of Holies.

Three hundred years had passed since that day. The custom of reading the law aloud to the people every seven years had been neglected. The people had broken God's law continually, partly because they were disobedient, and partly because they were ignorant of God's commands.

Josiah himself had never heard the law read. For the first time, he heard those terrible curses that would come upon the children of Israel if they should turn away from God to worship idols.

"If you will not do all the words of this law that are written in this book, then the Lord will make your sufferings severe. The Lord will curse and vex you in everything you attempt to do, until you be destroyed, because of your sin in forsaking Him.

"God will bring you and your king to a nation which neither you nor your fathers have known; and there shall you serve other gods, wood and stone. All these curses will come upon you until you are destroyed, because you did not listen to God's voice nor keep His commandments."

When Josiah heard the words of this curse, and realized that his people had done all the things that God had commanded them not to do, he tore his clothes in sorrow and fear. He sent the priest and the scribe and two or three others, to inquire of God about the curse.

The prophet Isaiah had been dead for a long time. His place had been taken by a prophetess, a woman named Huldah. Josiah's messengers went to her.

When they told her what they had come for, she said to them, "Tell the king that God will bring evil upon this kingdom and all its inhabitants. He will send all the curses that are written in the book which they have read before the king. Because the people have forsaken God and have burned incense to other gods, therefore the Lord will punish them.

"But because the king did humble himself before God, when he heard His curse, and wept in sorrow, therefore God has heard his cry. The king shall not see the evil that God will bring upon the kingdom; for He will wait until the king is dead."

When these words were brought to the king, Josiah called a great meeting of all the people — young and old. He read to them the words of the book which had been found in the Temple. Then King Josiah stood and made a solemn promise to serve the Lord. He made all the people promise that they too would serve God.

Part 2 — Josiah Picks a Fight

King Josiah started out to destroy thoroughly all the idols in the land, even more completely than he had done before.

First of all, he made the priests bring out of God's holy Temple all the dishes that had been made for the idol Baal, and for the worship of the sun and the moon and the stars. Josiah had these dishes burned, and their ashes carried away.

He had the houses of the witches pulled down, so that nobody could go to consult those people. It was one of God's commands that no witches should be allowed to live.

Then King Josiah went to a terrible place called Tophet. It was a valley where the people went with their little babies to have them burned to death in the arms of the idol Moloch. By filling this valley with abominable filth, King Josiah made it such a vile place that no man would ever go there to worship Moloch again.

Stabled near the Temple of God were some fine horses which one of the kings had given to the sun god when Judah was full of idolatry. King Josiah took away the horses and burned the chariots with fire.

On the Mount of Olives, across from Jerusalem, there were still some altars which King Solomon had made for his heathen wives. These idols and altars had been there on the Mount of Olives for four hundred years. King Josiah broke up all these old images. On the altars he burned the bones of dead men, so that nobody would ever want to sacrifice there again.

He went to Bethel, where there was left one of the golden calves which wicked King Jeroboam set up three hundred years earlier.

As King Josiah was standing in the graveyard at Bethel, directing his men to dig up men's bones to burn on the heathen altars, he saw a grave on the hillside with some writing over it. He asked, "What writing is that, that I see on that stone?"

The men of the city were able to tell him. "That is the grave of a prophet who lived three hundred years ago, and who foretold about these things which you have done to this altar."

This was true. Three hundred years before, when wicked King Jeroboam first made this altar for the worship of the golden calf, a prophet came to him and foretold that a king named Josiah, of David's line, would burn men's bones on that altar.

Josiah killed all the heathen priests that were in his kingdom, and burned their bones on the heathen altars, to pollute the altars so that no one would offer sacrifices on them.

If all the kings of Judah had been like Josiah there would have been no idolatry in the land. He turned to the Lord with all his heart and with all his soul and with all his might. He did everything that was in the book of the law of God.

Because Josiah was good and true to God, the Lord postponed the punishment that was coming to Judah for its wickedness. That punishment was coming, however. Josiah was the last actual king of Judah.

At the end of Josiah's life, Pharaoh-neco, king of Egypt, passed through the country on his way to the Euphrates River to fight with the king of Assyria.

At that time, Assyria and Egypt were the two greatest countries of the world. They were always fighting with each other, and they always passed through Palestine, because the land of the Israelites lay right in their way. Sometimes they had their battles there.

King Josiah wanted to fight with the Egyptian king. He called his army together and got ready for battle.

Pharaoh-neco sent word to Josiah, "I did not come out to fight with you. I only want to pass through your country to go and fight with my enemy, the king of Assyria." Then he added, "God has commanded me to fight against the Assyrians, and to hurry. Let me alone to do what God has commanded me to do."

But Josiah was determined to fight with the king of Egypt. He disguised himself in the clothes of an ordinary soldier, and went out and fought with Pharaoh-neco. In the battle, he was wounded.

Sorrowfully his servants put the wounded king into another chariot and carried him back to Jerusalem, where he died.

All Judah and Jerusalem mourned for good King Josiah. The men and women sang songs of mourning and affection for their beloved king. Jeremiah, the prophet, mourned with sad lamentations over him.

The people wanted Josiah's second son, Jehoahaz, to be king. The priests anointed him with oil to be ruler in his father's place.

CHAPTER 98

The Man Who Had to Prophesy

Jeremiah 1, 20, 36; II Kings 24; II Chronicles 36

Part 1 — People Who Hated the Truth

During the reign of Josiah, there was born in Josiah's kingdom a child who was to become a great and important man. His name was Jeremiah. He was the son of a priest.

When he was scarcely more than a boy, God spoke to Jeremiah, saying, "Before I made you, I sanctified you. Before you were born, I determined that you were to be a prophet to the nations. You are to be My prophet."

Jeremiah was frightened at these words. He said to God, "Oh, Lord God, I cannot speak, for I am only a child!"

But the Lord said, "Do not say you are only a child, for you are to go wherever I send you, and you are to say whatever I tell you to say. Do not be afraid of anyone, for I will be with you to keep you from harm."

In the time of Josiah, the people of Jerusalem turned to the Lord. After his death, when his son became king, they turned back again to their idolatry.

The sins of Judah had become so great that God could no longer let them go unpunished. Before sending a terrible punishment on the people of Judah, God sent the prophet Jeremiah to warn them and to try to persuade them to turn back to God.

The Lord said to Jeremiah, "Do you see what they do in the cities of Judah and in the streets of Jerusalem? The children gather wood, the fathers kindle the fire, the women knead their dough, to make cakes for the moon, whom they call the queen of heaven. They pour out drink-offerings to all sorts of gods."

Over and over again, God told Jeremiah to go and proclaim to the people of Judah their wickedness in leaving God to worship idols.

Already many of the people of Judah had gone into captivity. God commanded Jeremiah to stand in the gate of Jerusalem and to cry to the people who were left that unless they would turn from their wicked ways, God would bring severe punishment on them. If they would change, God would let them stay in their own land.

The people would not listen to Jeremiah. The Lord told the prophet to say to them, "If you do not repent, I will cast you out of my sight. A terrible nation shall come from the north and will take you away captive, as the people of Israel were taken captive."

The rulers of Judah were angry with Jeremiah, because he was continually prophesying to them of the evil that would come upon them. They warned him that they would kill him, if he would not stop.

But God promised to protect Jeremiah, and told the prophet to repeat the warning. If the people would not turn back to God, He would let them be carried away into captivity.

Because Jeremiah disregarded the wishes of the rulers and obeyed God, the priest punished him for his prophecies by putting his feet in the stocks — a wooden frame which held the prophet's feet so that he could not move.

For a whole day Jeremiah was left there. The stocks hurt his feet. Rude people came and laughed at him.

The next day he was set free. At first he said to himself, "I will not prophesy again in the name of the Lord." But Jeremiah found that he could not keep from speaking. God's word was in his heart, like a burning fire. He could not help prophesying.

Jeremiah's prophecies began to come true.

Jehoahaz was not a God-fearing king, as his father Josiah had been. He built himself a beautiful palace of cedar wood, painted bright scarlet. He made the workmen labor for nothing. He was not interested in his people, and did not take care of the poor.

The Egyptian king, Pharaoh-neco, whose soldiers had killed Josiah, came into the country of Judah and captured the king. They carried him off to Egypt and kept him there in prison for the rest of his life.

Pharaoh-neco made Jehoahaz' brother, Jehoiakim, king. He also forced the Israelites to pay him a big sum of money every year.

In this way the curses began to come true.

Part 2 — A Book That Was Burned

Jehoiakim reigned eleven years. Although he was a son of the good Josiah, he did all the evil things that the kings before him had done. He murdered people without cause and without remorse.

To punish this bad king and all the nation of Judah, God said, "I shall raise up the Chaldeans, a bitter and quick nation. They will march through the breadth of the land of Israel and possess it. Their horses are swifter than leopards and more fierce than evening wolves. Their horsemen shall come from far."

When Jeremiah brought this message, King Jehoiakim shut him in prison, so that he could not prophesy to the people.

The Lord commanded Jeremiah to take a roll or book, and to write in it all the prophecies that God had spoken to him since the beginning of his ministry.

Since Jeremiah could not go to the people, he sent for Baruch, who was a scribe or public writer. To him he spoke all the words that the Lord gave him. Baruch wrote down what the prophet said.

"Go to the Temple," Jeremiah said. "Read all the words you have written on this roll to the people who come to the Temple on the fast-day. It may be that they will turn from their sins and will pray to the Lord."

Very soon after that, a fast-day was proclaimed, and all the people of Judah came up to Jerusalem. Baruch took the roll that he had written from Jeremiah's dictation, and read it to all the people.

A man named Michaiah was very much interested in what Baruch was reading. He came to some of the princes and told them what he had heard. They sent for Baruch and asked him to read the roll to them also.

The princes were very much dismayed when they heard the words of Jeremiah's prophecies, that the Lord would certainly punish the people of Judah unless they would turn away from their evil ways. They exclaimed, "The king ought to know what this book says. We shall tell him about it. But you and Jeremiah must go and hide yourselves, lest the king kill you."

Leaving the roll safely hidden, they went to the king and told him about the dreadful punishment which Jeremiah said would come upon the people of Judah unless they would repent of their sins.

The king sent a scribe to get the roll and bring it to him. The scribe read aloud the prophecies, as the king sat in his beautiful winter palace before an open fire.

The king's father Josiah had torn his clothes in sorrow and fear when the book of the law, which had been found in the Temple, was read to him. But this king was not God-fearing. When the scribe had read three or four pages, King Jehoiakim scornfully took the book, cut out with his knife the leaves which had been read, and threw them into the fire. So he did with all the leaves, until the whole roll was burned.

Then the king commanded his soldiers to arrest Jeremiah and Baruch. But the Lord had hidden Jeremiah and Baruch, so that they could not be found.

God said to Jeremiah, "Take another roll and write in it the same words that were in the first roll. Say to Jehoiakim, 'You have burned this roll and refused its warning. Therefore you shall have no child to reign after you. Your dead body shall not be buried, but shall be thrown out to the heat of the daytime, and to the frost of the night!'"

Nebuchadnezzar stayed in this pitiable condition for seven years. Daniel 4

*God put it into King Cyrus' heart to allow
the Jews to return to Jerusalem.*   Ezra 1

CHAPTER 99

The Captivity of Judah

II KINGS 24; 25;   II CHRONICLES 36;   JEREMIAH 37, 38

PART 1 — THE KING OF BABYLON COMES

At last the time of punishment came for the people of Judah.

Meanwhile another nation had grown into power, the nation of Babylon (or Chaldea). Nebuchadnezzar, the king of Babylon, was a mighty man. He conquered Egypt and Assyria. He fought against all the surrounding countries and ruled over all the land from the Euphrates River to the Nile.

At last, he came with his mighty army against Judah. He conquered King Jehoiakim and put him in chains. In each land he conquered, Nebuchadnezzar made the king prisoner, and took him and all his people to far-away Babylon.

As Jeremiah had prophesied, Jehoiakim died and his body was thrown out to the heat of the daytime and the frost of night. No one cared enough about the wicked king to bury him. The people were too much frightened and excited by the things that were happening to think about him.

King Nebuchadnezzar made Jehoiakim's son Jehoiachin king over the people of Judah. He carried away some of the highest princes to be courtiers in his palace in Babylon.

The Babylonian king saw the splendid golden Temple that King Solomon had built so many years before. He admired its pure gold dishes, and he carried away a great many of them to the temple of his idol at Babylon.

This was the first time that King Nebuchadnezzar came to Jerusalem, but it was not the last. In three months he came again. This time he took the young King Jehoiachin, his mother, his wives, and his servants, and carried them all to Babylon. He took also the princes and soldiers, and all the men who were clever at making things. Ten thousand captives were carried away to Babylon.

Nebuchadnezzar also carried away the rest of the treasures of the temple and the palace. The beautiful golden dishes which were too large to be carried easily he broke in pieces.

The awful prophecies of Jeremiah came true. Mothers and fathers, old men and babies, were torn from their homes and sent to the far-away Babylon, a long, long journey over burning sands. The soldiers drove them on and treated them cruelly, so that many died on the way. The poor people plodded the seven hundred weary miles, weeping as they went.

Nebuchadnezzar left a few of the poorest of the poor in Jerusalem. They were not worth taking along. He made Zedekiah, the third son of good king Josiah, king of these people, at Jerusalem. And he made Zedekiah promise before God that he would not rebel.

But Zedekiah was a sinful man. He did not turn to God. Neither he nor his people would listen to Jeremiah. They did only evil in the sight of God.

When Zedekiah had been king for nine years, he rebelled against Nebuchadnezzar, although Jeremiah warned him that he should keep his promise.

Then Nebuchadnezzar came against Jerusalem again. He made forts outside the walls of Jerusalem and his soldiers besieged the city. The angry princes accused Jeremiah of being a friend of Nebuchadnezzar's soldiers, and they put him in prison.

For two years the army of Nebuchadnezzar besieged Jerusalem, until there was no food left and the people were starving. King Zedekiah sent for Jeremiah secretly and asked, "Is there any word from the Lord?" For he was greatly worried about the large army all around him.

Jeremiah answered him, "There is a message. God says that you shall be delivered into the hands of the king of Babylon."

Then Jeremiah begged the king not to send him back to the prison. And the king commanded that he should be kept in the prison yard instead of in the dungeon, and that bread should be given him each day as long as there was bread in the city.

Jeremiah spoke to the people, telling them not to fight against Nebuchadnezzar. He told them to give up. For God said that they would surely die by the sword, by famine, and by pestilence if they stayed in the city; but if they went out and gave themselves up, their lives would be spared.

Then the princes of Zedekiah were angry. They said to the king, "Jeremiah should be put to death. He weakens the people. He tells them to give up, and takes all their courage away."

Zedekiah was a weak king. He said, "Do what you will with him. I cannot stop you."

So the princes took Jeremiah and cast him into the king's prison. That was a deep pit in the cellar of the king's palace. They put ropes under his arms and let him down into the pit. There was no water there, but the bottom was all slimy mud. Jeremiah sank deep into the mud.

In the king's household there was a kind-hearted negro. He heard what happened to Jeremiah, and he went to the king to tell him, "The princes have treated Jeremiah shamefully. They have cast him into that awful dungeon, where he is likely to die."

King Zedekiah said, "Take thirty men and get him out of the dungeon."

The negro quickly called thirty men and went into the dark prison. He took some cast-off clothes and rags with him, which he threw down to Jeremiah. Then he called to him, "Put these under your arm-pits, so that the cords will not hurt you."

So they pulled Jeremiah up out of the pit. The king did not set him free, but kept him in the prison yard. There he could have air and sunshine. For God had promised to take care of him.

PART 2 — THE FALL OF JERUSALEM

While Jeremiah was in the dungeon, the long siege went on. The Babylonian soldiers still surrounded the city. Almost all the food in Jerusalem was gone, and the people were starving. Zedekiah was so proud that he would not follow the advice of Jeremiah to give himself up to the king of Babylon.

After a siege of two years, the Babylonian soldiers at last broke the wall of Jerusalem with their war machines, and poured into the city. When King Zedekiah and his princes saw that the soldiers had succeeded in battering down the strong walls, they fled secretly by night.

It was too late. The Babylonian soldiers saw them go. They chased after Zedekiah and his princes, and soon caught them. They took the king and his princes and his children, and brought them to King Nebuchadnezzar.

The victorious king did a most cruel thing. He had all the princes and all Zedekiah's children killed before his eyes. That dreadful sight was the last that Zedekiah ever saw on earth, for Nebuchadnezzar had his soldiers put out Zedekiah's eyes. The blind king was taken to Babylon and put in prison, where he had to stay all the rest of his life.

Then the soldiers came back to Jerusalem to destroy the city. They burned Solomon's beautiful golden Temple, the pride of the Jews, after taking out of it everything that could be carried away. All the golden spoons and dishes and candlesticks were taken away. The magnificent brass pillars which stood before the Temple were broken in pieces and carried to Babylon.

The soldiers burned all the magnificent houses of Jerusalem, and broke down the wall that had surrounded the city. As a final measure, King Nebuchadnezzar carried away most of the people who were still in the land, leaving only the very poorest.

At last the terrible judgment had come. The once splendid city lay in ruins. The walls were broken down, the houses were burned, and the golden Temple was a heap of ashes. The city lay desolate and deserted.

The soldiers put chains on Jeremiah to take him away with the other captives, but the king commanded that the prophet was to be set free, unhurt. He might go to Babylon with the captives if he desired; or he might stay behind with the few poor people who were left.

Jeremiah chose to stay in his own land. He sang sad lamentations about the fall of Jerusalem.

> "How doth the city sit solitary, that was full of people. . .
> She weepeth sore in the night, and her tears are on
>   her cheeks . . .
> Judah is gone into captivity . . .
> She dwelleth among the nations, she findeth no rest . . ."

The poor captives in Babylon also sang in their sadness:

"By the waters of Babylon,
   There we sat down, yea, we wept,
   When we remembered Zion . . .
How shall we sing Jehovah's song
   In a foreign land?"

While Judah was in captivity, Jeremiah continued to prophesy. He cried to the captive Israelites not to be discouraged. They were not to be cast off forever, as the ten tribes had been. After seventy years, God would bring them back again to their own country.

Although the people had forgotten God and had made it necessary for Him to punish them, He still loved them. He had said, "They shall be my people, and I will be their God." He loved Israel with an everlasting love, and He promised, "I will gather you out of all countries where I have driven you in My anger."

It was comforting to the poor captives in Babylon to know that after seventy years God would bring their children back to their own land.

Jeremiah brought a still more comforting message. He began to prophesy about the coming of the Christ, who was to be a blessing to the whole world.

Jeremiah also prophesied about the downfall of Babylon, which would come as a punishment for its cruelty and evil. These prophecies against Babylon were written in a book and given to one of the princes who went into captivity. When he reached Babylon he had to read all these words to the Jews there. Then he had to tie a stone to the book and throw it into the Euphrates River, saying as he did so, "So shall Babylon sink and shall not rise."

These prophecies about Babylon came true, for that city is so completely destroyed that it is difficult today to find even the place where it once was. Its magnificent palaces are nothing but heaps of ruins covered by drifting sands. Wild animals howl in the streets which knew the splendor of an imperial court. Babylon is indeed utterly desolate.

CHAPTER 100

Daniel

DANIEL 1, 2

PART 1 — THE BOY WHO REFUSED THE KING'S FOOD

When Nebuchadnezzar came up to Jerusalem for the first time, he commanded the master of his servants to go to Jerusalem and bring back some of the Jewish princes to be attendants at the palace in Babylon.

He was to choose young boys who were handsome and intelligent and well-mannered, and bring them to Babylon. There they were to be taught the Babylonian or Chaldean language, and to be trained in the manners and the wisdom of the land.

In due time the Jewish princes arrived at the king's court. Among them were four whose names were Daniel, Hananiah, Mishael, and Azariah. They were princes of royal blood. Very likely they were nephews of good King Josiah.

The king did not want the Jewish boys to keep their own names. They were given Chaldean names. Daniel was called Belteshazzar; Hananiah was given the name of Shadrach; Mishael was named Meshach; and Azariah was called Abed-nego.

King Nebuchadnezzar said that these princes must be healthy, as well as well-educated. He commanded that they should eat of the food which had been cooked for the king's table, and drink the kind of wine which the king himself drank.

This command worried the Jewish boys. Long ago, Moses had given very strict rules to the Jews about the kinds of food they might eat. They were permitted to eat only the animals that were called clean. Even those animals had to be killed in a certain way, so that no blood would be left in them. If these boys should eat the meat that the king sent them, they would surely break the law.

Daniel decided that he would not eat the king's meat, nor drink the wine that the king sent from his table. Although Daniel had been taken away from Judah when he was still young, he had made up his mind that he would be true to his God.

Daniel went to the master of the servants, who had charge of the food of the young princes, and asked if he and his three friends might be excused from eating the king's meat and drinking the king's wine.

Although these boys were far away from friends and family, God was with them. He made the master of the servants friendly. The man answered Daniel, "I would gladly let you eat what you like, but I am afraid that if my lord the king sees that you are looking paler and thinner than the other boys, he will cut off my head."

Daniel did not give up. "Will you let us try it for ten days?" he asked. "Give us vegetables to eat and water to drink, and then see if we do not look as rosy as the others."

So the master of the servants let them try it for ten days. At the end of that time, the four boys were fairer and healthier than any of the others, who had been eating the king's food and drinking the king's wine.

God rewarded the four boys who were true to Him by giving them knowledge and skill. Daniel came to have understanding in visions and dreams.

At the end of three years, the man in charge of the young Jewish princes prepared them to go in to see the king. He gave them perfume to rub on themselves, and he dressed them in handsome clothes. Then he took them in to the king.

By this time, the princes had learned to speak the Chaldean language very well. They had also been instructed in Chaldean manners, so that they knew how to answer the king when he spoke to them.

After all the princes had been brought in to the king and he had talked with them all, he chose Daniel, Shadrach, Meshach, and Abednego to stand before him. In matters of wisdom and understanding, the king found them ten times better than all the magicians and astrologers in his kingdom.

PART 2 — THE FORGOTTEN DREAM

One night Nebuchadnezzar had a strange dream. Like all heathen, this king was superstitious. He was afraid of dreams and signs.

In Babylon there were a great many magicians and astrologers, who made a business of explaining magic and dreams. King Nebuchadnezzar called together all these wise men and said to them, "I have dreamed, and I am worried about the meaning of my dream."

All the magicians answered, "O king, live forever! Tell us the dream and we will tell the king its meaning."

Nebuchadnezzar said to them, "I have forgotten the dream, but if you really are magicians, you will be able to tell me what it was. Unless you tell me the dream and its meaning, you will be cut in pieces, and your houses will be torn down to rubbish heaps. But if you will tell me the dream and its meaning, you will receive gifts and rewards, and great honor. Therefore tell me what I want to know."

The magicians trembled with dread as they heard this unreasonable demand. They knew that since Nebuchadnezzar had conquered all the world, he could do whatever he liked with them. He could kill them if he wanted, and nobody could lift a hand to help them. Every time he became angry his servants were terrified.

So the magicians answered tremblingly, "The king is asking us to do an impossible thing. No one could tell the king what he has dreamed, except the gods, who do not live on earth. No man can do it."

At this, the king flew into a rage. "You could tell me the dream, if you were real magicians. I know by this that you are not true wise men at all. You're pretenders. If you cannot tell the dream, how can I know that you can tell me the true meaning? Perhaps you just make up the meaning."

He turned to his soldiers. "Cut off their heads!" he ordered.

Throughout the city the captain of the king's bodyguard hunted for all the wise men — the magicians, the sorcerers, and the astrologers. The heads of Daniel and his companions were to be cut off too, for they were known as wise men.

Daniel asked the captain of the guard, "Why is the king in such a hurry to behead all the wise men?"

When he heard about the dream, Daniel went to the king. He was very brave to do this, for in those days no one dared to go into the room where the king was, unless the king first sent for him. If a man should come into the room where the king was, and the ruler should not hold out the golden scepter in his hand, that man was pushed out by the soldiers and killed.

Although Daniel knew this, he trusted in his God to keep him safe. The king held out the scepter, and Daniel came forward, bowing low to the ground. He said, "O king, live forever! If the king will give me time, I think I shall be able to tell him his dream."

When the king agreed to wait, Daniel went home. He and his three friends prayed to God that He would show them the king's dream, so that they would not be put to death, together with the other wise men.

God revealed the dream to Daniel when he was sleeping that night. Daniel thanked God, praising His kindness in showing him the dream. Then he went to the captain of the king's soldiers and said to him, "Do not cut off the heads of all the wise men. Bring me before the king, and I will tell him the dream and its meaning."

The soldier was very glad. He hurried to the king and said, "O king, live forever! I have found a man of the captives of Judah, who can tell the king his dream."

Then Nebuchadnezzar said to Daniel, "Are you able to tell me the dream and the meaning of it?"

"Yes," Daniel answered quietly. "It is impossible for the magicians and sorcerers to tell the king the dream which he himself has forgotten, but there is a God in Heaven who has sent a dream to the king to show him what will happen in the time to come.

"God has not revealed this dream to me because I am wiser than any living man, but in order that I may explain it to the king; for God wishes you to know the meaning.

"Your dream, O king, is this: You saw an image of great brightness and terrible appearance. The head of the image was of fine gold; his breast and his arms were of silver; his belly and his thighs were of brass; his legs were of iron; and his feet were partly of iron and partly of clay.

"In your dream you saw a stone, cut out of the mountain without human hands. This stone came rolling down the mountain. It bumped against the feet of the image, that were made of iron and clay, and it broke the feet to pieces. The iron and the brass and the silver and the gold were broken in small pieces, like fine dust. The wind blew them away. After that, the stone that broke the image began to grow until it became a great mountain which filled all the earth.

"This is the dream which you have dreamed, O king. Now I shall tell you the meaning of it.

"O king! You are a king of kings, for the God of heaven has given you a kingdom, and power, and glory. God has let you rule all the countries where men live. He has given you also the beasts of the fields and the birds of the air. You, O king, are the head of gold.

"After your kingdom shall come a kingdom of silver, not so powerful as yours. And after that, shall come a kingdom of brass, which also shall rule over all the world. Just as you saw that the feet and legs were partly of strong iron and partly of weak clay, so after these kingdoms there shall come a fourth kingdom which shall be partly strong, like iron, and partly weak, like clay.

"And just as you saw a stone, cut out of the mountain without the aid of human hands, which broke in pieces the iron and the clay, the silver and the gold; so the God of Heaven shall set up a kingdom which shall overcome all the others. It shall stand forever.

"The great God has made known to the king all these things which shall come to pass hereafter."

Nebuchadnezzar was very much astonished when he heard Daniel tell his dream and its meaning. He realized that there is a great God, much greater than his heathen idols, and that this great God brings to pass whatever happens. The king fell down on his face before Daniel and said, "Truly your God is a God of gods, and a Lord of kings, and a Revealer of secrets."

Nebuchadnezzar gave Daniel many rich presents. He made him ruler over the whole province of Babylon, and chief of the governors of the wise men.

Daniel did not forget his friends. He asked the king to make them rulers over the province. Daniel himself remained close to the king.

This wonderful dream that God sent to the great heathen king of Babylon came true in later days. After Nebuchadnezzar's kingdom, there came the kingdom of Persia; and after that, the kingdom of Greece; and still later, the Roman empire. In the days of the Roman empire Jesus Christ, the long-promised Savior of the world, was born. He began a kingdom of God which has spread over the whole world.

CHAPTER 101

The Fiery Furnace

DANIEL 3

PART 1 — "BOW DOWN TO THE IMAGE!"

We may be thankful that we live in these days, and not long ago, in the days of the Babylonian empire.

Today, in this country and in most of the countries of Europe, everyone can have whatever religion he thinks is right. But in the time of Nebuchadnezzar, the king could force any one of his subjects to pray to the god whom the king believed in.

The Jews were not the only people who had been carried away captive to Babylon. Nebuchadnezzar had taken people from many lands and brought them to his capital. All these people had their own gods, in whom they trusted.

The king thought that since each nation had its own god, the Jehovah of the Hebrews was only one of the more powerful. He himself worshipped an idol which he believed had made him the greatest king in the world.

Although Nebuchadnezzar had learned something about the God of the Israelites at the time of his strange dream, he was still a heathen.

He had learned the greatness of the God of the Hebrews, but he had not learned that Jehovah is the *only* true God.

One would naturally think that the Jews, who had been carried into captivity because they forgot God, would be happy to go on worshipping idols like the people around them. Strange to say, now that they were in a foreign country, they began to realize how foolish idolatry was. Their own religion seemed much more precious to them.

The prophet Jeremiah had told them that they were to return to their own land after seventy years of captivity. This was very comforting to the Jews. They became the more careful to keep their own religion, so that they and their children might not forget God.

Then something happened which made it hard for the Jews to worship their own God.

Nebuchadnezzar believed that the idol which he worshipped had helped him to conquer the world. To show his gratitude, the king had his workmen make a wonderful golden image of this god. The image was very high, and it was nine feet wide. The king had it set up in the plain, so that everybody could see it for miles around. When the sun shone on it, the image glistened and glittered with a glorious radiance.

King Nebuchadnezzar thought it would please his god, if all the conquered nations should be made to bow down to the image. Therefore he made a proclamation that all the rulers of the provinces of the kingdom of Babylon must come to the dedication of the image which the king had set up.

A herald was sent out with a trumpet. He cried aloud, "To you it is commanded, O people, that when you shall hear the sound of all kinds of musical instruments playing, you are to fall down and worship the golden image which Nebuchadnezzar has set up. Whoever does not fall down and worship, shall in the same hour be cast into the midst of a fiery furnace."

The people knew that the king would not hesitate to do as he threatened, if they should not obey. Therefore, when they heard the sound of all kinds of music, they fell down and worshipped the image.

Part 2 — Three Men Who Did Not Bow

Some wise men came to the king. They said to him, "O king, live forever! You have made a decree that every man who shall hear the sound of this music shall fall down and worship the golden image. Whoever does not fall down in worship shall be thrown into a furnace.

"Now, O king, there are certain Jews whom you have set over the province of Babylon. Their names are Shadrach, Meshach, and Abed-nego. These men, O king, have not obeyed you. They do not serve your gods, and they have not worshipped the golden image which you have set up."

No one had ever before disobeyed the king. All his subjects performed his slightest wish, because they were afraid for their lives. Nebuchadnezzar was astonished at the daring of these Jews. In his rage and indignation, he commanded his servants to bring the men before him.

When the three friends were brought to the great king, Nebuchadnezzar said, "Is it true, Shadrach, Meshach, and Abed-nego, that you do not serve my god, nor worship the golden image which I have set up?"

When they did not deny it, he continued: "I will give you one more chance. This time, if you worship the image which I have made, then all will be well. But if you do not fall down in worship, then in that very hour you shall be cast into the burning, fiery furnace. Your God is not powerful enough to save you from that place."

The three men bravely answered the king, "O King Nebuchadnezzar, we are not afraid to answer you. Our God is able to save us from you. We will not serve your gods, nor will we worship the golden image which you have set up. Even if our God does not save us from the fire, we still will not worship your golden image."

This defiant answer made the king so angry that his face grew stern and black with scowls. In his fierce anger, he commanded that the furnace should be heated seven times hotter than usual.

The strongest and biggest soldiers in the army bound the three men and cast them into the burning fiery furnace. Because the king had ordered the furnace to be made so hot, the roaring flames leaped out as the soldiers came near. The clothes of the soldiers caught the blaze, and they burned to death.

Men had been cast into this furnace before. It had been built for burning to death people whom the king wanted to punish. It was made so that the king could look into it and see the men burning.

Nebuchadnezzar watched as Shadrach, Meshach, and Abed-nego were cast into the furnace. Soon he saw something in the fiery flames that astonished him. He called to his wise men, "Were there not three men whom we cast into the midst of the fire?"

They replied, "True, O king! There were three men."

He cried in surprise, "I see *four* men, not bound, but free, walking in the midst of the fire. They are not burned nor hurt in the least. The fourth man looks like a god."

The king went to the door of the furnace and shouted aloud, "Shadrach, Meshach, and Abed-nego, come out, for I know that you are servants of the most high God."

So the three men came out of the furnace. The princes and wise men gathered around them, but there was no sign that they had been harmed. Their hair was not singed and their coats were not burned. There was not even the least smell of burning upon them.

The king exclaimed, "Blessed be the God of Shadrach, Meshach, and Abed-nego, who has sent His angel to deliver His servants who trusted in Him, and who have dared to risk their lives rather than worship any God except Jehovah.

And the king commanded that no one must speak anything against this God, but everywhere in his kingdom men must honor Him. For no other God, said he, can work such miracles.

How do you think the captive Jews felt when they saw that their God was able to protect His servants even in the burning furnace? It made them see that the idols of the heathen were useless, but their own God was powerful.

Many of the heathen, too, began to look with great respect upon the God of the Hebrews.

CHAPTER 102

The King Who Lived in the Fields

DANIEL 4

We have now come to a very remarkable chapter in our Bible. It is strange because it was written by a Babylonian king. Yes, it was truly written by that great ancient king, Nebuchadnezzar.

God put into the heart of the king the words he wrote, for God inspired all the authors of the Bible, and told them what to write. God made such a wonderful thing happen that Nebuchadnezzar wanted to tell all the world about it.

One day as Nebuchadnezzar lay at rest in his palace, he had a dream or vision which made him afraid. The dream troubled him so much that he ordered all the wise men before him, for he thought that they might be able to tell him its meaning.

The wise men appeared, but they could not tell the meaning of the dream. After all the others, Daniel came in and the king told him the dream.

Nebuchadnezzar had seen a very tall tree in the midst of the earth. It grew tall and strong, and the top of it reached to the sky, and it could be seen from all the earth.

Its leaves were green, and its fruit was plentiful, so that it gave food enough for all. The beasts of the field rested in its shadow, and the birds of the heaven lived in its branches.

"Then," continued the king as he told his dream to Daniel, "I saw in my visions that a watcher came down from heaven. He cried aloud, 'Chop down the tree, shake off its leaves, and scatter its fruit. Leave the stump of the tree in the ground, with a band of iron and brass around it. Leave it in the tender grass of the field, and let it be wet with the dew of heaven. Let his heart be changed from a man's heart to a beast's heart. Let seven years pass over him.

" 'This is to come to pass by the command of the holy ones, so that people may know that the most high God is the ruler of men, and that He gives the kingdom to whomsoever He will.' "

When Nebuchadnezzar told this strange dream, Daniel was astonished and shocked. He understood the dream. It prophesied what was going to happen to the great king, but that prophecy was so distressing that Daniel did not dare to tell the king. He stood silent before Nebuchadnezzar, not saying a word.

At last the king, who was watching Daniel's face, saw that he knew the meaning. He said to him gently, "Belteshazzar, do not be afraid to tell me what the dream means."

Daniel said, "My lord, the dream is so terrible and its meaning is so bitter, that I wish it were going to happen to your enemies instead of to you.

"The tree that you saw, which grew so strong and tall that it reached up to the sky and could be seen over the whole earth, which had beautiful leaves and plenty of fruit, which gave shade to all the animals — this wonderful tree is you, O king! You have grown strong, for your kingdoms reach to the end of the earth.

"You saw a holy watcher coming down from heaven, saying, 'Chop down the tree; but leave the stump of the tree in the earth, in the tender grass, and let it be wet with the dew of heaven. Let him live with the beasts of the field till seven years have passed by.'

"This is the meaning, O king!

"You will be driven away from men. You will have to live with the beasts of the field. For seven years you will have to eat grass like an ox and be wet with the dew of heaven, until you know that the most high God is the ruler in the kingdom of men, and that He gives power to whomsoever He will."

It was no wonder that Daniel had hesitated to tell the king this heavy news!

There was one thing which Daniel could say to the king which had some comfort for him. It was this: "In your dream, you saw that the holy one commanded that the root of the tree should be left in the ground. That means that you shall not lose your kingdom. After you have learned that God is the ruler over men, then your kingdom shall be given back to you again."

A whole year passed before the dream came true. One day, as the king was walking in the palace and looking at the splendid city of Babylon, he said to himself, "This is the great city that I have built, the great kingdom I have made by my power and for my honor."

As he spoke these boastful words, a voice came from Heaven, saying, "O King Nebuchadnezzar, the kingdom is taken away from you."

In that same hour, the dire punishment for his pride came upon the king. He suddenly became insane, so that the nobles of his palace drove him away into the fields, far away from men. He ate grass like an ox, and his body was wet with the dew of heaven. His hair grew like eagles' feathers, and his nails grew like birds' claws.

Nebuchadnezzar stayed in this pitiable condition for seven long years. "And at the end of the seven years," he wrote, "I lifted up my eyes to heaven, and my understanding came back to me. I blessed the most high God, and I praised and honored Him who lives forever, whose reign is everlasting, and whose kingdom is from generation to generation. He alone rules, and everything He does is right."

Nebuchadnezzar lived about a year after his reason returned. Once more he ruled his splendid kingdom, but no longer did he say. "This is great Babylon which I have built." Instead he praised God, for his heart was so wonderfully changed that he became a worshipper of Jehovah.

Nebuchadnezzar wrote his letter to all the people of the earth. His voice, proclaiming the greatness of God, has come to us, for it has become a part of the Bible.

CHAPTER 103

The Fall of Babylon

DANIEL 5

PART 1 — THE WRITING ON THE WALL

About thirty years after the death of Nebuchadnezzar, came a king whose name was Belshazzar. This new king did not serve God. He took away from Daniel the important positions which had been his in the time of Nebuchadnezzar.

After this king had reigned for several years, he gave a feast for a thousand of his lords in his splendid palace. The festival hall was so large that it could hold the party of a thousand men as they reclined together at the tables.

It occurred to Belshazzar to send for the golden and silver dishes which had been stolen out of the Temple at Jerusalem. His feast would be much grander, he thought, if he were to use the beautiful dishes which had been used in the service of the God of the Hebrews.

As the king and his princes drank the wine from the Temple vessels, they praised their own heathen idols. They thought that their gods of gold and silver had helped them to conquer the Israelites.

But as they were drinking, something strange happened. The fingers of a man's hand appeared on a wall, in the brightest spot, where a great candle was shedding its light.

Everyone in the great hall could see that hand. It showed plainly in the blaze of light. Everyone stopped drinking, and stared in amazement. A babel of questions arose. "What is it? What is it? How did it get there?"

While they gazed they grew dumb with fear, for the fingers began to write on the wall some words in an unknown language. No one knew what the words meant, but everyone felt that the message must be a dreadful one.

The king was panic-stricken. He knew that he had done wrong to take the treasures belonging to the Temple of the God of the Hebrews and to use them for his drunken feast. He was so dismayed that the joints of his legs grew weak. He staggered and almost fell. Finally he pulled himself together again, and commanded loudly, "Bring the astrologers and the magicians here quickly to read this writing."

To spur them on, he shouted, "Whoever can read this writing and tell me what it means shall be clothed in scarlet, with a gold chain about his neck, and he shall be made the third ruler in the kingdom."

All the wise men hurried into the banquet room. They looked for a long time at the writing on the wall, shaking their heads. None of them could read it.

King Belshazzar was more frightened than ever. His face turned white, and he shuddered with dread. Possibly he remembered how God had punished Nebuchadnezzar for his pride.

While they sat thus, numb with terror, the queen came into the banquet hall. She said, "O king, live forever! Do not be so frightened. There is a man in your kingdom in whom is the spirit of the holy gods. In the days of Nebuchadnezzar, there was found in this man knowledge and understanding of dreams. He was made the master of the magicians. Let Daniel be called, and he will show the meaning of this writing."

Daniel was sent for. The king asked him, "Are you that Daniel whom my father brought out of Judah with the captives? I have heard that the spirit of the gods is in you, and that you have understanding in dreams. The wise men and the astrologers have not been able to read this writing. If you can read it and tell me what it means, you shall be clothed with scarlet. You shall have a gold chain about your neck, and you shall be the third ruler in the kingdom."

"Keep your gifts," said Daniel, "or give them to someone else. I will read the writing to the king, and tell him its meaning."

Then Daniel interpreted the strange writing, saying, "O king! The most high God gave your father a kingdom and honor. All people obeyed the king. He did just as he pleased. But when he became proud, he was taken from his throne. He was driven from the sons of men, and he was made like the beasts. He was fed with grass like oxen, and his body was wet with the dew of heaven until he learned that God rules among men, and that He gives power to whomsoever He chooses.

"You knew all this, and yet in pride you opposed the Lord. You had your servants bring the vessels of the Lord's house for you and your lords to use in drinking wine. You have praised the gods of silver and gold. Your gods cannot see nor hear. They know nothing. It is Jehovah who gives you your life and all things that you have."

As Daniel spoke these stern words, the hand on the wall disappeared. Daniel told the king the meaning of the message.

"God has numbered your kingdom and finished it," he said; "You are weighed in the balances and found lacking. Your kingdom is divided and given to the Medes and the Persians."

Although the message was not pleasant, the king remembered his promise. He commanded his servants to bring a royal robe of scarlet for Daniel, and a heavy gold chain. The king stood up among his lords and proclaimed that Daniel was to be the third ruler in the kingdom.

PART 2 — THE PERSIANS ENTER THE CITY

After Daniel had interpreted the words which had appeared on the wall, the feast went on again; but no one felt like eating or drinking. The guests were talking about the writing on the wall. For they knew that danger was near.

A king named Cyrus had risen in the kingdom of Persia far to the east of Babylon. This new and powerful king was conquering all countries. First he had attacked his neighbor, the country of Media. Then he had marched against Babylon, Belshazzar's country, and had become master of that. Only the city of Babylon had not yet fallen, for its walls were high and strong.

The Persian king Cyrus had gone on conquering all the lands round about. His kingdom grew to be three times as large as Nebuchadnezzar's had been. Babylon alone defied him.

Cyrus gathered his soldiers around the high, strong walls of the city and besieged it. His men could not break down the walls nor climb over them. He had no hope that the people of the city would starve, for he knew they had enough food stored away to last for twenty years. They would never suffer from thirst, for the great River Euphrates ran under the walls, right through the city.

Behind their high walls, the people of Babylon felt perfectly safe. The lords were so sure that Cyrus could never get into the city that they had come to Belshazzar's feast without fear.

But while the feast was going on, the soldiers of Cyrus dug a new channel for the river, turning the water into a new river-bed. Along the empty channel, under the high walls, the soldiers of Cyrus crept quietly into the city.

At the feast, the people had seen the writing and had heard its meaning, and they were no longer gay.

Hark, what was the sound they heard? Could it be trumpets? And marching feet? Was it possible that the soldiers of Cyrus had found a way into the city?

As the sound of marching feet came nearer and nearer, the terrified nobles tried to escape from the banquet-hall.

It was too late. The palace was surrounded by the Persian soldiers. There was no escape. The guests were slain in the hall. Belshazzar, the king, died with them.

The warning which had so mysteriously appeared on the wall had come true. God had finished the kingdom, and had given it to the Medes and Persians.

An even older prophecy had come true at the same time. Many years earlier, Jeremiah had foretold the fall of Babylon. In this night the kingdom of Babylon was destroyed forever. It became a part of a far greater kingdom, ruled over by Cyrus the Persian, the greatest conqueror the world had ever seen.

CHAPTER 104

Daniel in the Lion's Den
DANIEL 6

PART 1 — THE JEALOUS RULERS

It was a happy day for the captive Israelites when the Persians took Babylon. These people were much kinder than the Babylonians had been, for they followed a noble religion, not at all like the idol-worship of the other heathen nations.

The founder of this religion was a man named Zoroaster. He lived alone in the mountains for twenty years, trying to find out truth by thinking.

He believed in only one great god, not in many idol-gods. He thought that this god had angels to help him. He also believed that there was a wicked spirit who had bad spirits to help him.

Zoroaster taught his followers to live well, for he was sure that there would come a judgment day when people would be punished or rewarded for the way in which they had lived.

It has been thought that perhaps this man got his ideas from the first Israelites who went into captivity. Even among the ten tribes who went into captivity because they worshipped idols there were some who were true to God. Perhaps Zoroaster had heard some of the captive Jews talking about the one great and good God, and about angels, and about Satan, and about a great judgment day. At any rate, these beliefs made the Persians better and kinder people.

The mighty Persian empire was too large to be ruled by one man alone. Cyrus put Darius, an old man of sixty-two years, on the throne of Babylon to rule that part of his empire for him.

Darius was an old man when he came to the throne. Only three years later he died. In that short time, something of great importance happened to Daniel.

Darius divided his kingdom into many smaller parts, and over these parts he placed princes. Over these princes he placed three presidents. And of these three presidents the Jew Daniel, the captive, was chief.

It was only natural that Daniel should be chosen for an important office. His wisdom was well-known, and so was his goodness. Even the scarlet robe which had been placed upon him showed that he was a person of rank.

But when Daniel, a Jew, was set over the other rulers, those princes became very jealous. They began to try to think of some way in which they could make trouble for him. They watched him to see if they could find any fault with his work; but Daniel was so faithful that they soon saw this was useless.

Finally they began to think of another way in which to make trouble for him. They knew that he was an earnest worshipper of his God. They said to each other, "The only way in which we can get the better of him is through his religion."

This is the trick which they planned:

All the princes went to King Darius. They said, "King Darius, live forever! All the rulers of the kingdoms have agreed to ask you to make a royal command that whoever shall pray to any man or god for thirty days, except to you, O king, shall be cast into the den of lions."

The king was pleased. He thought that his princes were trying to make his power known to the people. He never dreamed what was behind their request.

"Now, O king," said the princes, "make the decree and sign the writing, so that it may become one of the laws of the Medes and Persians, which cannot be changed."

Darius saw no harm in the law. All unsuspecting, he signed the decree.

PART 2 — THE GENTLE LIONS

All through his captivity, Daniel had remembered the prayer which Solomon had prayed at the dedication of the Temple in Jerusalem. God had promised that if in captivity His people should repent and pray towards the city which God had chosen, then He would hear their prayer.

Three times every day Daniel opened the windows of his room toward Jerusalem, kneeled down, and prayed to the Lord. Of course the princes knew this, and hoped by this means to get him into trouble.

Daniel soon heard what the princes had done. He knew that the writing was signed, so that it could not be changed, even by the king himself. He knew that what he was about to do meant certain death. Yet he went into his bedroom, where his windows were open toward Jerusalem, and he kneeled down and prayed to God.

The men who had persuaded the king to sign the law were delighted. "We've got him now!" they cried.

They hurried to the king and said, "O king, live forever! Did you not sign a decree that any man who prayed to any god or man except to you, for thirty days, would be thrown into the den of lions?"

The king replied, "That is true. It is part of the law of the Medes and Persians, which cannot be changed."

"O king, live forever!" answered the rulers triumphantly. "That Daniel, one of the captives of Judah, does not obey your decree. He prays to his God three times each day!"

Darius, when he heard this, was very, very sorry that he had done such an unwise thing as to sign that decree. He knew that Daniel was a good man. He spent the whole day in trying to find a way to save Daniel.

The rulers came to the king again and said, "You know, O king, that it is a law of the Medes and Persians that no decree signed by the king may be changed."

The king knew that. He knew he could do nothing to help Daniel. The law had been signed and could not be changed. The king commanded that Daniel be brought in. He spoke very sorrowfully to him. "Your God, whom you serve so well, will deliver you."

The king's soldiers opened the mouth of the lions' den and threw Daniel down into it. A great stone was laid upon the opening. The king unwillingly put his own seal upon the stone so that no one might move it.

In sorrow of heart the king went to the palace. He would eat none of the rich food that had been prepared for him. When the musicians came in to play for him as usual, he sent them away.

At last Darius went to bed, but he did not sleep. All night long he tossed from one side to the other. No sleep for Darius that night!

Meanwhile, the men who had caused Daniel to be thrown to the lions went home in great good humor. "That's the end of Daniel," they said to each other. "He will never trouble us again."

And how did Daniel spend the night? Did the hungry lions tear him limb from limb?

Daniel was safe. God did not let the lions hurt His servant, or even frighten him. An angel came down from Heaven to shut the lions' mouths.

Very likely the lions came and rubbed themselves against Daniel; and when he petted them, they purred with pleasure, like great pussy-cats. Perhaps they lay down and let Daniel rest against their soft bodies. Perhaps he spent the night in sleep. He knew that he was perfectly safe.

As soon as the gray dawn came peering through the windows of the palace, the tired king, who had not slept a wink all night, arose and dressed and hurried to the lions' den. He was pale with weariness and anxiety. Had Daniel's God been able to save him from the hungry lions?

As soon as he reached the den, the king cried in a mournful voice, "Daniel, O Daniel, servant of the living God, is your God, whom you serve continually, able to deliver you from the lions?"

He waited anxiously. Would he hear only the roar of savage lions in answer?

Clear and strong came back the voice of Daniel, "O king, live forever! My God sent His angel and shut the lions' mouths, so that they have not hurt me."

The king was very glad. He commanded that Daniel should be taken out of the pit. Then he commanded his servants to bring those men who had plotted against Daniel and to cast them into the den. The hungry lions sprang at those men, even before they reached the bottom of the cave.

King Darius became convinced that the God of Daniel must be the one about whom Zoroaster had taught. No one else could do such marvellous things.

He made another decree, far better than the first. In it, he commanded all people everywhere to worship the God of Daniel, who had saved His servant from the power of the lions.

Daniel became an important man in the kingdom, for God was with him. At the death of Darius three years later, the great Cyrus came to the throne, but Daniel still prospered.

God sent Daniel some visions of things that were going to happen in the future. He sent an angel to tell Daniel that God loved him and would always be with him, because of his faith.

CHAPTER 105

Back to the Promised Land

EZRA 1, 2; ISAIAH 44, 45

PART 1 — THE PERSIAN KING TO WHOM GOD TALKED

Daniel was a mere boy when he first came as a captive to Babylon. He lived at the court through the reign of Nebuchadnezzar, which lasted for forty years. After this king came one or two others, and then Belshazzar, and then Darius.

When Cyrus came to the throne after the death of Darius, Daniel was a very old man. Seventy years had passed since he came to Babylon as a captive. If he was fifteen years old at that time, he must now have been about eighty-five years old.

Daniel had held very high positions in the kingdom. He had been in desperate danger many times, but God had wonderfully saved his life.

At the beginning of the captivity, the prophet Jeremiah wrote a letter to the captive Jews, telling them that after seventy years God would bring them back to their own country.

The seventy years had now passed. God had not forgotten His people. He had already planned their return, which was brought about in a most unexpected way.

No sooner had Cyrus become king, than God put into his heart the desire to let the Jews go back to Jerusalem. Even more surprising, King Cyrus offered to help them to rebuild the Temple which had been destroyed.

This is what the king wrote:

PROCLAMATION OF CYRUS TO THE JEWS

The Lord God has given all the kingdoms of the earth to me. He has commanded me to build Him a house in Jerusalem, which is in Judah.

Now, let all His people go up to Jerusalem, and build the house of the Lord God of Israel, for He is the true God.

If there are any who do not go up, let them help those who do go, with silver and gold, with food and with beasts to travel on.

How astounded the Jews must have been when they read this proclamation posted on the street corners! Could it possibly be true that they were to go back to Jerusalem to rebuild the Temple? They could hardly believe it.

Excited meetings were held on the streets and in the houses. The people were so happy that they danced and sang, shouting and clapping their hands. One of their poets wrote a song about it which you can read in Psalm one hundred twenty-six.

This proclamation was all the more wonderful for this reason: One hundred fifty years before Cyrus was born, Isaiah had prophesied about him. Isaiah had mentioned Cyrus by name, and had told just what he would do.

Isaiah had known all this because God told him what to say. God knows everything that will happen, even to the end of the world, because He is the one who makes everything come to pass. He is the ruler of all the world.

The Bible does not tell us that Cyrus knew about this prophecy, but Daniel probably told him about it. How astonished and awed Cyrus must have felt when he read that the God of the Hebrews had said:

"Cyrus is My shepherd, and he shall perform all My pleasure. He shall say of Jerusalem, 'She shall be built.' He shall say of the Temple, 'Your foundation shall be laid.' "

Isaiah had also written these words: "Cyrus is My anointed one. I have guided his right hand so that the nations might be subdued before him."

How astonished the king must have been, to read the words which God addressed directly to him: "I will go before you, and will make the rough places smooth. I will break in pieces the doors of brass, and cut apart the bars of iron. I will give you the treasures of darkness and the hidden riches of secret places, so that you may know that it is Jehovah, the God of Israel, who calls you by name."

When Cyrus read these prophecies, he must have understood why he had been so great a conqueror. It was not by his own power or might, but by the help of God.

Perhaps, too, he read this promise: "Look unto Me and be saved, all the ends of the earth; for I am God and there is none else."

PART 2 — THE WORK ON THE TEMPLE

With glad hearts, the Jews began to get ready for the long journey to their own land.

It was more than five hundred miles to Jerusalem. Even today that is a great distance. At that time it was much longer and harder.

At the end of the journey, the people would find the Temple destroyed and the houses in ashes. Jerusalem had been in ruins ever since it was burned by Nebuchadnezzar, seventy years before. Not a single house had been left standing. Clearing away the rubbish and building new houses would take at least a year. During all that time the Jews would have to live in tents.

For this reason all the Jews were not able to go back to Jerusalem. Some had a grandfather or grandmother who was too old to stand hard travel and rough living conditions. Some had little babies who could not live through the long journey.

Daniel was one of the many Jews who did not go. He was at least eighty-five years old. He could not have endured the long journey, nor the rough life the Jews would have to live while they were building the city.

Only the youngest and strongest men and women went back. The people who stayed in Babylon helped the others with money, with goods of all kinds, and with animals to travel on.

King Cyrus helped them, too. He gave back to them all the golden and silver platters and basins which Nebuchadnezzar had taken out of the Temple of Jerusalem. These things had been very carefully kept in a heathen temple, for they were valuable. King Cyrus had his treasurer count them and give back every single dish — five thousand four hundred of them.

The travellers were very heavily loaded for their long journey. Besides the rich treasure of the Temple, they carried household goods with which to begin housekeeping.

Fifty thousand people made the journey back to Jerusalem. Most of them had to walk, for the camels and asses carried the vessels of the Temple and the household goods. The people could easily walk twenty or thirty miles in a day.

As they went, the men and women sang. This made the journey pleasant and cheerful. In the evenings, they took the tents from the backs of the camels and set them up on the warm sand. They made little bonfires and cooked their suppers. As they lay down to sleep, they said happily, "We are one day nearer home."

At last they reached their own country. They found the ruins of the Temple. It was nothing but a heap of rubbish. After clearing off the rubbish, the Jews built an altar there, where they offered sacrifices each morning and evening.

Each family began to look for the plot of land which Joshua had given to their fathers. While in captivity in Babylon, they had been very careful to keep a family record, so that they would know, when they went back to Judah, where they were to live. Each man settled down on the land which had belonged to his fathers.

After they had been in Jerusalem for a year, and had made themselves places to live, they began to build another Temple. On the day when the foundation was laid, they had a joyful meeting. They praised the Lord, singing together the song of David, "Because He is good, and His mercy endureth forever toward Israel."

Many of the old priests and Levites, who remembered the first Temple before it had been burned, wept; for they knew that the new Temple could never be as glorious as the first had been. It was impossible to tell the noise of the shout of joy from the noise of the weeping of the old men. There was a commotion of shouting and weeping which could be heard a long way off.

CHAPTER 106

The Rebuilding of the City

EZRA 4, 5, 6

PART 1 — QUARRELSOME PEOPLE WHO STOPPED THE WORK

As you remember, the ten tribes of Israel were taken into captivity by the king of Assyria. That king then brought foreign nations into Samaria to fill up the land.

These strangers lived in Samaria all the seventy years while the Jews were in captivity in Babylon. Now when they saw that some of the Jews had come back from the captivity and were building up the Temple, they came to the high priest.

"Let us help you build up the Temple," they offered. "We have worshipped your God ever since we came to this country."

But Zerubbabel and the rest of the elders of Israel refused. They knew that the Samaritans did not worship God truly, since they worshipped idols at the same time. They replied, "You have nothing to do with us in building a house to our God. King Cyrus has commanded us to build it."

This answer made the Samaritans very angry. Instead of helping the Jews, they did everything that they could to hinder them.

Meanwhile, King Cyrus had died, after a short reign. Another king ruled for a little while. After him came another king.

Knowing that the Jews no longer had King Cyrus to protect them, the Samaritans wrote a letter to this new ruler. This letter said, "Let it be known to the king that the Jews who have come here to Jerusalem are building up that rebellious city. They have already finished the walls and joined the foundations.

"If this city is built up again, the people will not pay their taxes to the king. Let the records of earlier kings be searched. It will be found that this city has always been a bad city. That is the reason it was destroyed."

The king sent a letter in answer to the Samaritans. "Your letter has been read to me," he wrote. "I commanded that search be made in the old records. It has been found that Jerusalem was always a bad city which rebelled against its rulers. I command that these Jews stop building their city until I tell them they may go on."

When the Samaritans received this letter, they hurried as fast as they could to Jerusalem. There was nothing for the Jews to do but to lay down their tools and stop work. Their dreams were not yet to come true.

As long as this king ruled, the Jews did nothing to the unfinished Temple. They were so discouraged that they did not think of protesting.

It was not long before this king died. After him there came a king named Darius. This second Darius was a very great ruler — even greater than Cyrus had been. His kingdom reached from India to Egypt. He ruled his kingdom wisely and well. He is called Darius the Great.

God spoke to two prophets and gave them a message to the Jews. God wanted them to go on building the Temple.

To encourage them, God said, "Those of you who saw Solomon's Temple, know that this Temple is as nothing compared to it. But some day I will fill this second house with glory. The glory of this latter house will be greater than the glory of Solomon's Temple."

How was God going to fulfill this promise?

You remember that God told Abraham and Isaiah and many of His prophets that some day He would send a man who would be a blessing to all the world, and would save it from sin. God now told the prophets to say to the Jews, "It is only a little while till I shall send this Savior. He is called 'the Desire of all nations'. It will be the glory of this Temple that the Savior will come into it."

With renewed courage the Jews went on with their work on the Temple. They began to look forward to the coming of the promised Savior as they had never done before.

They went back to their work on the temple with new determination.

Ezra 6

"*O king, let my life be given me, and the life of my people.*" Esther 7

PART 2 — A DECREE FROM PERSIA

As soon as the Jews began to build their Temple again, the same quarrelsome Samaritans came up to make trouble once more.

"Who told you to go on building this Temple?" they asked. "We will tell the king what you are doing, if you do not stop."

But the Jews would not stop this time, for God had commanded them to go on building. Seeing that they could not make the Jews stop, the Samaritans wrote another letter. It was addressed to Darius the Great, who was king now.

Long before this, writing had become quite common. Many people understood how to write. All the kings had scribes who wrote accounts of the events that happened in that king's reign. These writings were stored away in the king's library, so that later rulers could read what had been done.

This is the letter which the troublesome Samaritans wrote:

"Unto Darius the king, all peace!

"Be it known to the king that we went to Jerusalem, to the Temple which the Jews are rapidly building. We asked them who commanded them to go on building the Temple, and they answered,

" 'We are the servants of the God of Heaven, and we are building the house that was built many years ago by a great king of Israel. Our fathers made God angry, and He let King Nebuchadnezzar come and carry them away captive, and destroy the Temple. But King Cyrus, in the first years of his reign, made a decree to build this temple again. He sent us back here and told us to build it.'

"Let the king's servants make a search in the king's library, and see if it is true that Cyrus did as these people said."

When Darius received the letter, he commanded his servants to search in the library where the rolls were laid up, to see if such a record could be found.

Without any trouble, there was found a roll which said, "In the first year of Cyrus, he made a decree about the Temple of God in Jerusalem. This was the decree:

" 'Let the house be built and let the foundations be strongly laid, with three rows of great stones, and a row of new timber. Let the cost be taken out of the king's money.' "

When King Darius found this roll in the library of records, he wrote to the Samaritans these words:

"I, King Darius, command that you let these Jews alone. Let them go on building the house of their God. Help them with money, and with goods, and with everything that they need. Take the money out of the king's treasuries. Give them also young bullocks, rams, lambs, wheat, salt, wine, and oil, and whatever they need for offerings. These things are to be given every day, so that the Jews may pray for the life of the king and his sons.

"And I also make a decree that if anyone shall change this law, timbers shall be pulled down from his house, and he shall be hanged on the gallows made of those timbers."

The Samaritans obeyed this command. Instead of hindering the Jews, they helped them, as the king had said they should do. They were afraid to do anything else, after the dreadful punishment which the king threatened.

So the children of Israel built the Temple and finished it. In all, the work took about twenty years. After it was all finished, they dedicated the Temple. They offered hundreds of bullocks, rams, and lambs. They set up again the service of the priests and Levites, as Moses had commanded.

Last of all, they celebrated the Passover with great joy. For the Lord had made them glad by making King Darius want to help them build another house for the Lord.

CHAPTER 107

Esther, The Beautiful Queen

ESTHER 1, 2

PART 1 — THE FEAST THAT LASTED A WEEK

We have now come to a very interesting story of what happened to some of the Jews who did not go back to Judah.

Although fifty thousand Jews had returned, there were many who stayed behind for some reason. These people were scattered throughout the great kingdom of Persia. Wherever they went, they carried the knowledge of their great God with them.

At the time of our story, Darius the Great was dead. His son Ahasuerus, or Xerxes, ruled over the empire. King Ahasuerus was not a wise and God-fearing man, as his father had been. He was foolish and weak.

The capital of the empire had been removed to another city. The splendor of Babylon had been destroyed. Its wonderful walls, three hundred feet high, had been broken down. The hundred gates had been carried away. The whole city was in ruins.

Shushan, the new capital, was even more magnificent than Babylon had been. King Ahasuerus lived there in great splendor. From that city he ruled his mighty empire, which stretched from India in the far east to Ethiopia, south of Egypt, in the west — a country as big as the United States.

In the third year of his reign, Ahasuerus invited the princes and nobles of all the provinces of his kingdom to a feast in Shushan.

What a wonderful gathering it was!

There were princes from India, magnificently dressed in rich embroidered silks ablaze with glittering jewels — diamonds, rubies, and pearls. They rode in state in curtained chairs perched high on the backs of elephants.

There were wild-looking Arab tribesmen from Arabia who seemed to fly along on their swift horses, heavy silver chains dangling from their necks as they rode.

From Ethiopia came black negroes, wearing enormous turbans on their heads, and bearing splendid gifts for the king. Many more princes, from all parts of the empire, came at his command.

For half a year King Ahasuerus entertained this great assembly of princes in his city, showing them all the splendor of his kingdom. At the end of this time he gave a feast to all the people of the city of Shushan. Young and old, rich and poor, great and humble — all were invited.

The garden of the palace was beautifully decorated for the occasion with festoons of violet and white and green wreaths, fastened with purple and white ribbons to silver rings in the marble pillars. The ground was paved with red, blue, white, and black marble. There were couches of gold and silver for the guests to recline upon. An abundance of wine was served in gold and silver cups.

The feast in the garden was attended only by the men of the city, for at that time and in that country men and women never gathered together. No lady ever came into a room where men were or ever walked on the street without first covering her face with a long veil.

While the king was entertaining the men of the city in the garden, his wife, Queen Vashti, was giving a feast for the women inside the palace. For a whole week this celebration lasted, and everyone was very gay. Yet trouble was soon to come.

PART 2 — A JEWISH GIRL BECOMES QUEEN

On the seventh day of the feast, King Ahasuerus, who had drunk far too much wine, sent seven of his servants into the hall where the queen was entertaining the women. He told the servants to bring the queen out to the garden, wearing the royal crown on her head, so that the people and the princes might see her beauty.

If the king had not been drunk, he would never have made this demand. He would have known that the queen was too modest to come out into the garden with her face uncovered, to be stared at by the crowd of men.

The servants came back and reported that Queen Vashti had refused to come out with them. The king was furiously angry. He consulted his seven wise men and asked, "What shall be done to Queen Vashti, because she refused to obey the king's command?"

Everyone was desperately afraid of the king, for he had the power to strike off the head of anyone who did not please him. His servants trembled whenever they saw him in a drunken temper.

Therefore the seven wise men, although they knew that the queen was right, tried to soothe the king by agreeing with him that she deserved punishment.

They said, "The queen has done wrong not only to the king, but to all the princes and the people as well. All the ladies of Media and Persia will refuse to obey their husbands when they hear of this.

"If it please the king, let him make a royal decree, saying that Vashti shall be queen no longer because she has disobeyed. Let the king give the crown to another lady, who is more obedient than she. When all the people of the kingdom hear how Vashti has been punished, then all the wives everywhere will obey their husbands."

King Ahasuerus was pleased with this advice. To all parts of the empire he sent letters written in the common language of the country, saying:

EVERY MAN SHALL BE RULER IN HIS OWN HOUSE
BY ORDER OF THE KING

The servants then said to the king, "Let officers be appointed in all the provinces of the kingdom. Let them gather together the most beautiful young girls of the empire. Let these girls be brought to the palace, and the maiden which pleases the king shall be queen instead of Vashti."

The king thought this was a good idea. He commanded his servants to begin to hunt everywhere for lovely young girls.

Now it so happened that in the city of Shushan there lived a Jew named Mordecai, who had a beautiful young cousin, Esther. Since her father and mother were dead, Mordecai had brought her up as his own daughter.

Esther was chosen as one of the young girls who were brought to the palace so that the king might pick a new queen from among them. She did not mention that she was a Jew.

Many beautiful girls from all parts of the empire were brought to Shushan. After living in the palace for a while, each one appeared before the king. When Esther finally came before Ahasuerus, he loved her more than all the others. He set the royal crown on her head, and made her queen in the place of Vashti.

Every day Mordecai walked before the court of the women's house and sat in the palace gate to find out how Esther was. While he lingered about the palace, he discovered a plot which two servants had made, to kill the king.

Mordecai told Esther what he had heard, so that she might warn Ahasuerus. The plot was proved, and the two men were hanged. What Mordecai had done was written down in the records of the kings of Media and Persia, but the king forgot to reward the man who had saved his life.

CHAPTER 108

Queen Esther Saves Her People

ESTHER 3-9

PART 1 — A PRINCE WHO HATED THE JEWS

There was one man, named Haman, whom the king liked better than all his other princes. Haman was given many honors which the other nobles did not receive.

Whenever Haman walked or rode out of the king's palace, all the servants and princes were obliged to bow low, with their faces to the ground. Haman walked proudly between these rows of men. He thought himself more important than anyone else on earth.

Mordecai alone did not bow down when Haman passed. The servants who were in the king's gate said to the Jew, "Why do you not obey the king's command to bow down to Haman?" And when they could not make him bow down, they told Haman.

Haman was furiously angry. He began to think of some way to punish Mordecai.

Because Haman was the king's favorite, he could easily have had Mordecai hanged. But he thought that to kill Mordecai was not severe enough. He scorned to lay hands on this man alone. He had been told that Mordecai was a Jew. Nothing would satisfy him, except to destroy all the Jews in the kingdom.

This he did not dare to do without the king's permission. There were thousands of Jews in the kingdom. Every year they paid the king a great amount of taxes. If the Jews were all killed, the king would lose much money.

And if the king should not happen to be pleased to have all the Jews murdered, he might turn on Haman and have his head cut off for asking such a thing.   These kings might be very fond of a man one minute, and the next minute order him beheaded.

Like all heathen, Haman was very superstitious. He did not dare to ask the king for this favor, until he had first cast lots to find the lucky day.   In that country, where everybody believed in luck and signs and dreams, there were men whose work it was to cast lots. Haman had these men cast lots for him daily, till they should find a lucky day for him to go to the king to get permission to kill all the Jews.

Every day was unlucky for Haman. And every day, for a whole year, Haman went to the magicians, to see if the lot had come up.

At last, after a year, the lot was favorable.

When Haman went to the king, he did not say that he was furious with Mordecai, because the Jew would not kneel down to him and do him honor.   He knew well enough that King Ahasuerus would never let him kill thousands of people for such a reason.

He said, instead, "O king, live forever. There is a certain people scattered abroad among the nations, in all the provinces of your kingdom.   Their laws are different from the laws of all other peoples. They do not keep the king's laws; therefore it is not for the king's profit to let them live.   If it pleases the king, let it be written that they be destroyed.   I will pay ten thousand talents into the king's treasury, so that the king will not lose any taxes by having them killed."

Haman was an extremely rich man. Ten thousand talents of his money would be about fourteen million dollars today.   But, although Haman had a great deal of wealth, King Ahasuerus had still more. With all the provinces bringing him huge sums in taxes, he was far richer than any king in the world today. So he said to Haman, "Keep the silver. You may have the people too. Do whatever you like with them."

The king gave him his royal ring, with the king's seal on it. Haman could write anything he pleased and sign it with the seal in the king's ring. When it was signed with the king's ring, it would become a law of the Medes and Persians which could not be altered.

Oh, how happy Haman was! The lot had spoken truly. It was certainly a lucky day for him!

Haman gathered all the king's scribes, or secretaries. He told them to write to all the governors that ruled over the provinces of the empire. This was what they were to write:

THE KING'S DECREE!
ON THE THIRTEENTH DAY OF THE TWELFTH MONTH, YOU ARE TO KILL ALL THE JEWS, BOTH YOUNG AND OLD, LITTLE CHILDREN AND WOMEN.

Riders on swift camels went out in every direction to carry the news to the farthest bounds of the king's great dominions.

Haman sat down to drink with the king. Outside the palace, the city of Shushan was in great distress. Could anything save the Jews from this terrible fate?

In every land where the king's message came, there was weeping, wailing, and mourning. This terrible message meant that all the Jews in the world were to be killed at the end of the year. Even those in Judah, who had just finished building their Temple, were to be killed.

Since they first began to be a nation, the Jews had never been in such danger. If Haman's plot had succeeded, there would not be one Jew in the world today.

Could anything save them?

Part 2 — The Brave Queen

When Mordecai heard that all the Jews were to be killed, he tore his clothes, put on sackcloth and ashes, and went out into the middle of the city, raising a loud and bitter cry.

He came in front of the king's palace and wept at the gate. He could not enter, for no one clothed in sackcloth was allowed to go into the palace.

Queen Esther did not know about the scheme that Haman had made. Some of her maidservants, however, told her that Mordecai was outside the gate, lying in sackcloth and ashes.

Esther, not knowing what it was all about, sent Mordecai some good clothes to wear instead of those that were torn and covered with ashes. Mordecai sent them back again.

Esther became alarmed. What could be the matter with Mordecai? Was someone in the family dead? She sent one of her servants to ask Mordecai what was the matter. Why was he dressed in mourning?

Mordecai told the servant the whole story of Haman's plot. He gave the servant a copy of the decree to show to the queen. Mordecai asked Esther to go in to the king, and beg him not to let her people be killed.

Esther was frightened when she heard this message. She told the servant to say this to Mordecai: "All the king's servants and the people of the court know that any man or woman who shall come into the inner court without being called is almost certain to die. He is put to death, unless the king holds out the golden scepter as a sign that he may live. I have not been called in to the king for thirty days. How could I go to see him?"

Mordecai knew the danger. But he knew, too, that the Jews were in dreadful danger.

He sent her another message, saying, "Do not think that you will be saved when all the Jews are killed, just because you are the queen. If you say nothing to the king, then the Jews will be saved in some other way, but you and your family will be killed. Who knows whether you have not been made queen just for such a time as this, so that you can save your people?"

Esther was panic-stricken when she thought of going in to the king without being called. But she bravely decided that she would try to save her people, even if she lost her life in the attempt.

This was her answer to Mordecai: "Gather all the Jews in the city. Fast for me, neither eating nor drinking for three days. My maidens and I will do the same. Then I will go in to the king. And if I perish, I perish."

After three days, Esther put on her royal dress, and stood in the inner court of the palace. Her heart almost stopped beating as she waited. But when the king saw his beautiful young queen, he smiled and held out the golden scepter that was in his hand.

Esther came in and touched the tip of the scepter. The king spoke kindly to her. "What do you wish, Queen Esther? What is your request? It shall be given you, even to the half of the kingdom."

Esther was far too frightened to tell the king at once what she wanted. She answered, "If it seem good to the king, let the king and Haman come to the banquet which I have prepared today."

The king was very much pleased. He said to some of his servants, "Tell Haman to make haste, so that he may come to the queen's banquet."

At the banquet, the king asked Esther again what she wanted; for he knew that there was something troubling her.

But Esther was still afraid to tell him. She said, "My request is this: If I have found favor in the sight of the king, and if it please the king to grant my request, let the king and Haman come again tomorrow to another banquet which I shall prepare for them. I shall tell the king tomorrow what I desire."

When Esther postponed telling the king what she wanted to ask, of course he became very curious and eager to know what it could be.

Haman went home with a joyful heart. He was proud to think that he, and he alone, had been invited with the king to the queen's banquet. But as he went out of the gate, all his joy left him, for he saw that the Jew, Mordecai, did not bow down to him.

Haman went home and called his family and his friends around him. He reminded them how rich he was, how many children he had, and how the king had promoted him above all the other princes.

Last of all he said, "Esther, the queen, let no man come in with the king to the banquet which she had prepared, except myself, and tomorrow I am again invited with the king to the queen's banquet. Yet all these honors that I have received amount to nothing, as long as I see Mordecai sitting at the king's gate."

Seeing that Haman was so disturbed, his wife and friends said to him, "Let a gallows be made, seventy-five feet high. Ask the king for permission to hang Mordecai on the gallows. Then you can go merrily to the banquet with the king."

This suggestion pleased Haman. He caused the gallows to be made that very afternoon. He watched it going up higher and higher. He thought how greatly he would enjoy seeing his enemy hanging up there.

PART 3 — HAMAN'S REWARD

The king could not sleep that night. He commanded one of the servants to bring the book of records of his reign.

In this book it had been recorded that Mordecai once discovered a plot of the king's servants to murder King Ahasuerus. As the servant read this to the king, Ahasuerus asked, "What reward has been given to Mordecai for this?"

"Nothing has been done for him," the servant replied.

The king made up his mind to reward Mordecai. He asked, "Who is in the court?"

"Haman is standing there," his servants told him.

Early as it was, Haman had just come into the outer court to ask the king to let him hang Mordecai on the gallows which had been built the afternoon before.

"Let Haman come in," the king ordered. After his favorite had entered, the king asked, "What shall be done to the man whom the king delights to honor?"

Haman thought in his heart, "To whom would the king like to show honor more than to myself?"

So he immediately thought of the thing that he would like most of all to have done to himself, and he said, "Let the servants bring clothes which the king is accustomed to wear, and also the horse that the king rides upon, and the royal crown. Let this apparel be delivered to one of the king's most noble princes, that with these things they may array the man whom the king delights to honor. Let him be led on horseback through the city, and let the prince proclaim before him, 'Thus shall it be done to the man whom the king delights to honor.'"

"Make haste," the king replied, "Take the horse and the apparel, and do what you have said to Mordecai, the Jew, who sits at the gate. Let nothing fail of all that you have said."

Haman's bitter disappointment cannot be described. He had supposed that he was the one who was to wear the fine clothes and the crown, and to ride on the king's horse. Now he found that he was the one to lead the horse; and his hated enemy Mordecai was the one to ride in state!

He had to obey the king. He dressed Mordecai in the king's rich garments. He put him upon the king's splendid horse, which was dressed in gold and silver trappings, and led him through the streets of the city. As he went, he shouted, "Thus shall it be done to the man whom the king delights to honor."

Everybody in the street bowed low to Mordecai as he rode along. Oh, how it pained Haman to see that! He was the one to whom the people had always bowed — and now they were bowing to his hated enemy! And *he* was the servant who had to lead the horse through the streets!

After the procession was over, Haman was so filled with shame that he did not dare to look up. He went home, mourning and having his head covered.

He told his wife and all his friends everything that had happened. While he was still talking with them, the king's servant came to take him to the banquet that Queen Esther had prepared. Haman had forgotten all about it in his shame.

During the banquet, the king again said, "What is your petition, Queen Esther? It shall be granted. What is your request? It shall be given to you, even to the half of the kingdom."

Esther clasped her hands. With a piteous look in her eyes, she fell upon her knees and said, "If I have found favor in your sight, O king, and if it pleases the king, let my life be given to me at my petition; and my people's life at my request. For we are sold, I and my people, to be destroyed."

When the king heard the pleading words of his beautiful queen, he sprung up, flaming with anger. "Who is it who has dared to do such a thing?"

Esther, turning, pointed to Haman. "The enemy is this wicked Haman," she said.

Choking with anger, the king arose from the banquet. He strode out into the palace garden to work off his wrath.

Haman in terror stood up to beg Queen Esther for his life. When he saw how angry the king was, he realized that he was in very great danger.

The king returned from the garden. Haman, in his fear and anguish, had fallen upon the couch where Esther was. That made the king more furiously angry than ever. He burst out, "How dare he touch the queen?"

Some of the servants who saw how angry the king was, and who knew that the king would command Haman to be put to death, covered Haman's face with a cloth. One of them volunteered, "There is a gallows, seventy-five feet high, that Haman made for hanging Mordecai, who is the king's friend. It is standing in the garden of Haman's house."

"Hang Haman on that gallows," commanded the king.

Haman was immediately taken out and hanged upon the gallows which he had made for Mordecai.

Esther told the king all about the cruel plot that Haman had made. She also told him that Mordecai was her cousin, who had brought her up like a father. The king sent for Mordecai and gave him the ring which he had once given to Haman. He made Mordecai the highest officer in the whole kingdom of Persia.

PART 4 — A TIME OF REJOICING

Haman was dead, but the harm that he had done still lived on. The decree had gone out to all countries that on the thirteenth day of the twelfth month, all the Jews were to be destroyed. This was a law of the Medes and Persians which even the king could not change.

Esther came to see the king once more. She fell down at his feet, begging him with tears to undo the mischief that Haman had done.

The king held out his golden scepter again to Esther. She stood

Malachi wrote the very last book of the Old Testament. Malachi 1

up, saying, "If it pleases the king, and if I have found favor in his sight, let there be made a law to change the letters which Haman wrote in order to have all the Jews destroyed. How can I endure to see this evil happen to my people?"

The king answered, "Haman has been hanged upon the gallows, but the writing cannot be changed, because it is a law of the Medes and Persians. But I will give Mordecai permission to send another message to all the Jews."

So the king called in many writers. Mordecai had them write letters to all the provinces. These letters were written in the king's name, and sealed with the king's ring. They were sent hastily by the king's swift riders.

This is what the letters said:

PROCLAMATION

On the thirteenth day of the twelfth month, according to the first proclamation, all the Jews were to be destroyed. The king hereby gives the Jews permission to gather themselves together, and to fight against all those who want to hurt them. They may defend themselves, and kill all who try to kill them.

In every town in the great empire, little and big, a copy of this proclamation was posted in the market-place. There were no newspapers in those days, nor telephones, nor telegraphs, nor radios. But I do not suppose that there was one person past babyhood in all that vast empire, who did not know about those two proclamations posted up side by side in the market-places.

The first was Haman's notice sent out in the king's name that all the Jews were to be destroyed.

Beside Haman's proclamation was Mordecai's letter also sent out in the king's name that the Jews in every city should gather themselves together and fight for their lives; and that they should destroy all those who tried to hurt them.

The Jews in all the king's dominions had nine months to prepare for the fateful day. When at last it came, they gathered in all their cities. All the rulers of the provinces helped them. The Jews overcame all their enemies, and hanged the ten sons of Haman on the gallows that their father had made. Many of the people of the land became Jews.

The Jews rested on the next day. They made it a holiday, a time of feasting and gladness.

Meanwhile, Mordecai had become a great man. He was clothed in royal apparel of violet and white, and he wore a great crown of gold upon his head. As time passed, he advanced to even greater power, becoming the king's right-hand man.

He wrote to all the Jews, telling them that the fourteenth and fifteenth days of the month should be celebrated each year in memory of the terrible days when the whole race of the Jews had been in danger of being destroyed.

These two days were called the "Feast of Purim." Even to this day the Jews keep that feast every year in remembrance of the time when the Jewish race was saved from destruction.

CHAPTER 109

Ezra, The Teacher of the Law

EZRA 7-10

PART 1 — THE SECOND COMPANY OF PILGRIMS

There was a Jew living in Persia who had spent all his life in an earnest study of the law of God. His name was Ezra. Besides studying the Scriptures himself, Ezra taught the law of God to other Jewish people. For this he was known all over Persia, even to the king.

God gave this learned man the desire to go to Judah and to teach the holy law of God to the people who had gone back there.

Ezra asked the king to let him go to Judah for this purpose. The king was very kind. He not only let Ezra go, but he said that any Jews who wanted to go with him might do so. Besides, the king and the nobles of Persia gave Ezra a splendid present of gold and silver, and of beautiful gold and silver dishes for the Temple. The gold and silver which was given to Ezra amounted to more than three million dollars. This treasure was to be an offering to the great God.

King Artaxerxes promised to pay all Ezra's expenses for the Temple out of the king's treasury. Like Cyrus and Darius, this king believed in the great God of Heaven, and thought he ought to honor Him.

At the time when the Israelites were carried away to Babylon by Nebuchadnezzar, it was a punishment for them; but it turned out to be a great blessing for the world. The Jews had worshipped idols; yet when they found themselves captive in a heathen land, they gave up their idolatry and turned back to their own God. Thus they had a good influence on their heathen neighbors.

Through the Jews, Nebuchadnezzar had seen God's power. When Daniel was able to tell the king the forgotten dream about the image with feet of clay, Nebuchadnezzar was deeply moved. All the people, as well as the king, were filled with wonder when God kept Shadrach, Meshach, and Abed-nego safe in the fiery furnace where they had been thrown for refusing to worship the golden image.

Afterwards, when God humbled the great Nebuchadnezzar by making him insane for seven years, the king said when he recovered; "Now, I, Nebuchadnezzar, praise and honor the King of Heaven." The people, too, began to believe.

Perhaps Nebuchadnezzar did not give up his heathen gods altogether, but he did at least learn about Israel's true God.

In Belshazzar's time, God showed His power in the hand-writing on the wall; and in the time of Darius by saving Daniel from the lions.

Later, when Cyrus the Persian and Darius the Great reigned, these kings sent the Jews to Jerusalem, and helped them build their Temple. They gave money and animals for sacrifice, asking the Jews to pray to the God of Heaven for them and their sons.

Now, when Ezra went back to Jerusalem with his band of Israelites, the king gave all kinds of provisions for the service in the Temple.
The nobles, too, sent rich gifts of money and of gold and silver dishes.
The king gave Ezra authority to set up judges over the people, and to
teach the Jews the law of God, and to require them to follow that law.

So the captivity of the Jews, while it was a punishment for them,
was a great blessing to the heathen peoples. Many who had never before heard of God turned to Him. In Queen Esther's time many men
learned to fear God. And the knowledge of God was never again
wholly lost in these countries, for we know that the wise men who
came to see the baby Jesus came from these lands.

PART 2 — EZRA IN JERUSALEM

About six or seven thousand people returned to Judah with Ezra.
For three days the company camped by the side of a river. There
before they had actually started, Ezra proclaimed a fast. They spent
the time in prayer, asking God to guide them, and to take care of them
and their little ones in the long and dangerous journey.

Before them lay seven hundred miles of hot desert country where
they were almost certain to meet with wild robber bands. Ezra says,
"I was ashamed to ask the king for a band of soldiers and horsemen
to help protect us, because we had said to the king, 'Our God will take
care of us.' So we fasted and prayed to God to take care of us, and He
listened to our prayer.

"And I found that there were no priests with us; so I sent back
to ask some priests to come with us, so that we could have some minis-
ters for the house of our God. Two hundred fifty priests and Levites
joined our band. I chose twenty-two of the priests, and I gave them
charge of the silver and the gold and the dishes that the king and his
lords had offered."

So the pilgrims started on their long journey. Four months later
they reached Jerusalem. It was now eighty years since the first group
of Israelites had returned from Persia. Most of those who had made
the first journey were dead.

As soon as Ezra reached Jerusalem with his band, they delivered all the gold and silver to the Temple, and offered sacrifices for a burnt offering to the Lord.

Very soon after Ezra came, princes of the first group came to tell him that many of the first Jews had again married heathen wives. They had forgotten God's command not to mingle with the heathen. Even some of the princes and rulers were guilty.

Ezra was so horrified when he heard this that he tore his clothes, and mourned all day. Others felt sorrowful, too, and sat with him, mourning.

It was no wonder that Ezra was horrified, for the people had just suffered captivity because of their idolatry. If they were going to marry heathen wives, they would soon drift back again into heathenism. Then God would punish them yet more severely.

Ezra mourned all day. In the evening he fell down upon his knees and spread out his hands, praying to the Lord. He said, "O my God, I am ashamed, and blush to lift up my face. We have sinned — our sin is so great, that it has reached up to the heavens. What shall we say? We have forsaken Thee. If we again break Thy commandments, wilt Thou not be angry with us, and consume us?"

While Ezra was praying and weeping, a very great company of men, women, and children came together, weeping because of their sins.

One of the men said to Ezra, "Come and let us make a promise to God that we will send away all our heathen wives."

So they called a meeting. It was arranged that all the men who had taken heathen wives must come at appointed times to Ezra the priest, and to one or two other chief men. After due judgment, the guilty men would have to send away their heathen wives. Thus they honored God and put away idolatry.

CHAPTER 110

Nehemiah, The Governor of Jerusalem

NEHEMIAH 1, 2, 6, 8; MALACHI 3, 4

PART 1 — WHY THE KING'S SERVANT WAS SAD

In Persia there was a rich Jewish nobleman named Nehemiah, who held the high office of cup-bearer to the king. This position was a very important one. It was given only to some very trustworthy person. The cup-bearer had to taste every cup of wine that he handed to the king so that no one would have a chance to poison the king.

One day a man who had been in Judah, came back to the royal city of Persia. He brought bad news. "The people in Jerusalem are in great trouble," he said. "The walls of the city are broken down, and the gates are burned."

When Nehemiah heard this news, he felt very sorrowful. As he went about his work he kept praying to God to help Jerusalem. His sadness showed in his face.

The king noticed that his cup-bearer looked unhappy. "Why do you look so sad today?" he asked. "You are not sick; so this must be sorrow of heart."

Nehemiah was afraid, for servants should never look sad in the presence of the king. Yet he ventured to say, "Let the king live forever! Why should I not be sad, when the city where my fathers are buried lies waste, and its gates are burned with fire?"

The king asked graciously, "What can I do to help you?"

This was the very same king who had sent Ezra back to Jerusalem about fifteen years earlier with a company of six or seven thousand people, and a treasure of gold and silver for the Temple. This fact, and the king's gracious words, gave Nehemiah new courage.

"If it pleases the king, and if I have found favor in his sight," Nehemiah replied, "I would ask that you would send me to Judah to the city where my fathers are buried, so that I may build it up."

"How long do you want to stay, and when will you come back?" the king asked.

"Twelve years," was the answer. Then Nehemiah asked the king to give him letters to the governors of the countries beyond the Euphrates River, so that they would let him go through their countries safely. Nehemiah also received a letter addressed to the keeper of the king's forest, directing him to give the Jews timber to build the wall of the city and a palace for the governor.

Besides writing these letters for Nehemiah, the king gave him a company of soldiers and horsemen. For he had to pass through wild country.

Nehemiah reached Jerusalem safely. After a day or two of rest, he and a few other men mounted horses, and went all around the city of Jerusalem by night, to see in what condition it was.

They found that the city was in very bad shape. The walls were broken down, and the gates had been burned. There were great empty spaces without houses where heaps of rubbish had lain ever since Nebuchadnezzar burned the city.

This desolate condition distressed Nehemiah very much. The next day, he came to the rulers of Jerusalem and said to them, "You see how bad the condition of Jerusalem is. The city lies waste, and the gates have been destroyed by fire. Let us build up the walls of the city."

The rulers were eager to begin the work. Nehemiah gave orders, since the Persian king had made him governor. He portioned out the wall all around the city. Each family was given a part of the wall nearest its own house to build.

Some of the Samaritans, living in the city or near by, made trouble for Nehemiah. They laughed scornfully at him for trying to build up the walls.

One of them said mockingly to his soldiers, "What are these feeble Jews doing? Where will they get the stones to build the wall? Will they dig them out of the heaps of burned rubbish?"

Another said disdainfully, "Such a wall as they are building! Why, even if a fox should go up, he would break it down!"

Instead of answering this mockery, Nehemiah cried to God, saying, "Hear, O our God, for we are despised!"

The Jews went on building the wall. They worked earnestly, and soon the work was almost finished. When the Samaritans heard that the walls were really going up, they became the more disturbed. They planned to come and fight against Jerusalem, to hinder the work.

The Israelites prayed to God. Nehemiah placed the people behind the wall, with swords and with spears and with bows. He said to them, "Do not be afraid of them; remember that our Lord is great and strong. Fight for your sons and your daughters, your wives and your houses."

When the enemies of the Jews discovered that their plan of attack was known, they realized that they were beaten.

Nehemiah wrote: "Then we returned to the work of building the wall. From that time on, I divided my people. Half of them went on building the wall, and the other half held weapons, so as to be ready to fight in case of an attack.

"Those who built on top of the wall, and those who carried mortar and other burdens, worked with one hand, carrying a weapon in the other hand. Each of the builders had a sword by his side. The man who sounded the trumpet was close by me.

"I said to the nobles, 'The work is great, and we are separated upon the wall, one from another. In whatever place you hear the sound of the trumpet, gather quickly to that place. Our God will fight for us.'

"At the same time I said to the people, 'Let every one with his servant remain in Jerusalem all night, to be a guard to us at night.' For there were many men working upon the wall who lived not in Jerusalem, but in some of the nearby towns. Neither I, nor my brothers, nor my servants, nor the men of the guard which followed me — none of us put off our clothes at night, for we were always prepared to fight.

"The king had appointed me to be governor. For the twelve years that I ruled, I did not accept any salary, because the people were poor. Moreover, I fed many of the people at my own expense."

PART 2 — JERUSALEM FINALLY REBUILT

"Now it came to pass," wrote Nehemiah, "that when the Samaritans heard that I had almost finished the wall, they tried another way to hinder me. They said to me, 'Come and let us meet together in one of the villages.'

"But I sent messengers to them, saying, 'I am too busy. I am doing a great work, and cannot come down. Why should the work stop while I leave it to come down to you?'

"They asked me four times, but I did not go. The fifth time, they sent a man with a letter which said, 'It is reported among us that you are building the wall so that you can make yourself king in Jerusalem. If you do not come down to us, we will tell the king of Persia that you intend to make yourself king here.'

"I sent word to them, 'We are doing no such thing as you say. You are making up that story in your own heart.' And I prayed to God.

"At last the wall was finished. It took fifty-two days to complete it. When all our enemies heard that the work was done, they were afraid, for they saw that it was God's doing."

Nehemiah had done a remarkable thing in getting the wall completed in less than two months. He had worked hard, and the people had helped him with all their might.

The next thing that Nehemiah did, was to gather all the families that had come back from Babylon. He found an old book that contained a list of all the true Jewish families. He looked up the record in this book to find out if there were any among them who were not true Jews.

This was a long task, for there were forty-two thousand people. When it was finished, it was found that the family names of some of the priests were not mentioned in the book. Those priests were not allowed to serve in the Temple any longer.

Nehemiah and Ezra called the people to a great meeting. Ezra stood up on a high wooden platform that had been made for that purpose, and blessed the Lord, the great God. The people answered, "Amen, Amen!" and they bowed their heads to the ground and worshipped the Lord.

Ezra and his helpers read from the book of the law of God. They explained the meaning of what was read, so that the people would understand the law. From morning to noon they read. The people listened attentively. As they listened, they wept, for it was a long time since they had heard the law of their God. Perhaps many of them who had come out of Persia had never heard the law read.

Then Nehemiah, the governor, and Ezra, the scribe, said to the people, "This day is holy to your God. Go home and have a feast. Eat the fat and drink the sweet, and send food to the poor. Do not mourn, for the joy of the Lord is your strength."

So all the people went home to eat and to drink, and to have a happy holiday. They were glad to return to the worship of God.

On the next day the people came together again. Again Ezra read from the book of the law.

It was found in the law of Moses that the children of Israel were commanded to dwell in arbors to celebrate the feast of the seventh month. The Jews went to the Mount of Olives and cut olive branches, pine branches, and palm branches. They made arbors on the roofs of their houses and in their gardens.

The people were happy to think that they were again becoming true Israelites. They no longer wanted to be like the heathen nations, as before the captivity. They had been completely cured.

Ezra read daily out of the law of God. The people made a solemn promise to God to walk in His law, and to keep all His commandments.

While Nehemiah was governor, there lived a prophet named Malachi. He wrote the very last book of the Old Testament.

Malachi told the people that the promised Savior was soon coming. He said, "Unto you that fear My name, shall the Sun of righteousness arise." He also foretold the coming of John the Baptist, saying, "Behold, I sent you Elijah, the prophet."

To comfort the people who tried to serve God, Malachi said, "Then they that feared the Lord spoke one with another. Jehovah hearkened and heard it, and a book of remembrance was written before Him, for them that feared Jehovah and that thought upon His name. 'And they shall be Mine,' says Jehovah of hosts."

That is a comforting thought. Those who love God, and who often meet together to talk about Him, are the ones whom God will call His own. That is one of the lessons that all study of the Bible teaches us. God loves those who serve Him, and He will always be with them.